Viking Olver Eriksen

Sunken Nuclear Submarines

Viking Olver Eriksen

Sunken Nuclear Submarines

A Threat to the Environment?

Norwegian
University Press

Norwegian University Press (Universitetsforlaget AS), 0608 Oslo 6
Distributed world-wide excluding Scandinavia by
Oxford University Press, Walton Street, Oxford OX2 6DP

London   New York   Toronto
Delhi   Bombay   Calcutta   Madras   Karachi
Kuala Lumpur   Singapore   Hong Kong   Tokyo
Nairobi   Dar es Salaam   Cape Town
Melbourne   Auckland

and associated companies in
Beirut   Berlin   Ibadam   Mexico City   Nicosia

British Library Cataloguing in Publication Data
Eriksen, Viking Olver
   Sunken nuclear submarines.
   1. Nuclear powered submarines. Sinking. Environmental aspects
   I. Title
   359.933

   ISBN 82-00-21019-7

Printed in Norway
by A.s Verbum, Stavanger

Contents

Preface

Nuclear submarines are at present indispensable instruments in maintaining the strategic balance between the superpowers. They are well suited for launching intercontinental ballistic missiles. They hide easily in the oceans, they are almost impossible to detect and can reach any point on the globe with their deadly weapons. This book, however, is not about the strategic importance of nuclear submarines or about their weaponry. Their contribution to the preservation of global political stability is acknowledged, but does it have a price? That depends –.

So far, seven nuclear submarines have sunk and five of them are still resting on the seabed as technological refuse. The public displays growing unease about the potential dangers posed by the frequent accidents in the North Atlantic. Whenever a major accident with a nuclear submarine occurs, the authorities give comforting statements that there is nothing to worry about. There is no spread of radioactive materials and the reactor propulsion plants remain sealed.

No leakage has in fact been observed from the seven sunken submarines. But even if there had been leakages, this would not have meant the end of the world. The reassuring statements may well be the truth – but they are not the whole truth. Firstly, how close are we to experiencing leakages? Those who know, if they ever know, tell nothing. That is classified information. Secondly, what if the next submarine should sink in relatively shallow waters close to populated areas or on fishing banks during the spawning season? We do not even know whether that problem has been considered. And, thirdly, what state of preparedness should be built up to meet the next accident?

Some countries are more vulnerable than others to the potential consequences of a nuclear submarine accident. Norway is one of them.

As a NATO country, Norway is highly interested in allowing allied marine forces to display their strength in the Norwegian Sea. The 16 Soviet marine bases on the Kola Peninsula serve as home bases for about 125 nuclear submarines, 2 nuclear-propelled cruisers, 6 nuclear icebreakers and 1 civilian nuclear cargo ship. The density of nuclear-propelled ships in the Norwegian Sea is therefore high. The three most recent Soviet nuclear accidents admitted by the Soviet authorities took place within the short span of 3 1/2 months in the Norwegian coastal areas: In April 1989 a *Mike* class submarine sank south of Bear Island with the loss of 44 men; a leakage occurred in the primary cooling circuit of an *Echo II* class submarine on June 25th, 100 kilometers northwest of the island of Senja in North Norway; and on July 16th an *Alfa* submarine had problems in her nuclear propulsion plant in the Barents Sea, 120 kilometers east of Vardø. A fourth accident seems to have occurred in December 1989, not yet admitted by the Soviet authorities. All these incidents have reminded the public that the potential dangers are not just vague theoretical fantasies. They are realistic examples of what might, and most probably will, happen again, and then, maybe, with more serious consequences.

It stands to reason that the public has a right to be reasonably well informed about the potential risks of nuclear submarines. There are risks involved in the operation of any weapon or weapon carrier. There is a price to pay for security, which has to be accepted. The difference between nuclear submarines and probably any other weapon is that the damage caused by a submarine accident is not limited to what happens there and then. Secondary long-lasting consequences might be considerable. If this view is incorrect, those who know better should explain the true picture in a way which can be subject to independent verification.

It is understood and accepted that sensitive military information has to be kept secret. Operational characteristics of the nuclear propulsion plants, their reliability and endurance are essential factors for judging the combat power of a submarine. Vital information can, however, be generalized sufficiently to disguise design details while still giving the public an understanding of what is at stake. Authorities in countries that have nuclear ships patrolling along their coasts should have a minimum of preparedness in case of an accident. But they hardly know what to prepare for.

The nuclear powers should address themselves to the public in the matter of safety of nuclear submarines. To preserve the present positive attitude to the prevailing nuclear strategy, which concerns all of us, the public should be made to understand that there might be a price to pay. If the price is very low, so much the better. But let us know. Each of the countries concerned have performed extensive safety assessments of their nuclear submarines, including safety at their home bases. The military self-interest in obtaining a high degree of operative safety is obvious. Unsafe submarines will never be effective weapon carriers.

Parts of the risks involved should be disclosed. Do the safety assessments include evaluations of the consequences of releases of radioactive materials from sunken submarines? Are there any reasons why security considerations should prevent making such assessments public? In fact, the potential consequences of the spread of releases from a sunken submarine could well be studied jointly by the nuclear powers. An international agreement on the surveillance of the sunken nuclear submarines should be established. This is not different from the practice already adopted for the study of releases from dumping sites for radioactive waste in the North Atlantic. These releases have been extensively studied by various international groups of experts. What is needed is a continuation and amplification of this work.

This book is intended for members of the public who want to know more about the risks involved with nuclear submarines. The book raises more questions than it answers. Next to nothing has been published on nuclear propulsion plants for submarines and their safety issues. It has been necessary to resort to information on old civilian nuclear cargo-ships, Soviet ice-breakers and generic information from the civilian nuclear power industry. This situation reminds us of the drunken man in the dark who has dropped his door-key and who stubbornly keeps searching beneath the nearest street-light because the light is better there.

'Resorting to the nearest street-light' has been a guideline in writing this book. It is therefore inevitable that the presentation has its shortcomings. Those who are in a freer and better position to expand on the subject should feel an obligation to do so.

Part one

The issues –

About 80 nuclear submarines are continuously patrolling the North Atlantic Ocean and connected seas. They are powerful instruments of the current strategic balance between the superpowers. However, they represent a far from negligible safety risk which has to be weighed against the benefit of increased political security.

The United States and the Soviet Union concluded in 1972 an Agreement on the Prevention of Incidents On and Over the High Seas. This agreement requires the two navies to observe strictly the International Regulations for Preventing Collisions at Sea and is a reflection of the superpowers' mutual interest for risk reduction at sea. Reduction of safety risks of nuclear submarines at sea deserves to be raised to the same level of international considerations.

The recent dramatic political changes in Eastern Europe have already had a profound influence on the disarmament negotiations between the superpowers. The British journal The Economist *has proposed a reduction in the number of land-based nuclear missiles from 10 000 to 2 000 for each of the superpowers. The Economist would like to see the United States abolish its land-based missiles entirely and put most of them into submarines. This would entail a considerable expansion in the number of nuclear submarines. If this is the price to pay for an overall reduction in the strategic nuclear forces, so let it be – but it is a blank cheque.*

The safety of the nuclear submarines is solely the responsibility of the Nuclear Powers and outside the realm of public scrutiny. Should it be so? A large number of accidents have actually occurred involving nuclear submarines. More will come. Are we prepared?

1. An overview

From 1954 to 1988 about 200 accidents involving nuclear powered submarines have been reported. 50 of them relate to ballistic missile submarines and the other 150 to attack and cruise missile submarines, ref.
1. On the other hand, the US Naval Safety Center has reported 190
mishaps with nuclear submarines in the Atlantic during the period 1983
to 1987 (ref. 23). Fig. 1 shows these mishaps divided into major categories by cause. It is not known how serious these mishaps were.

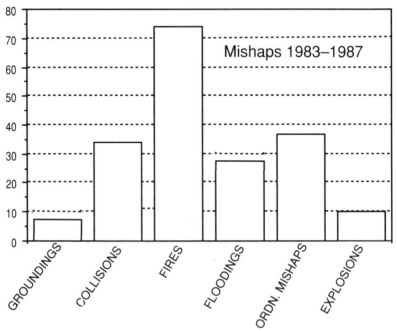

Fig. 1 Submarine mishaps in the Atlantic, 1983–1987 (Naval Safety Center).

Accidents will happen with all human activity. No one will doubt that the responsible naval authorities are doing their utmost to improve the safety of the submarines and their propulsion plants. The gravity of a major nuclear submarine accident, however, has an additional dimension parallelled only in biological and chemical warfare. The consequences for marine life might be considerable if an accident should happen in the wrong place at the wrong moment.

Substantial effort is invested in technology to improve safety and reduce the likelihood of experiencing a large accident. But what is being done to increase the 'preparedness' for the next accident? The very basis for being prepared against 'something' is information about what this 'something' is.

Sunken nuclear submarines

Six nuclear submarines have sunk in the North Atlantic. Two are American, the other four are Soviet. Five are still resting on the seabed. One has been salvaged. In addition, one Soviet nuclear submarine has sunk in the Pacific. She has also been salvaged.

The American nuclear submarine *Thresher* went down on April 10, 1963 at a depth of 2 500 meters, 350 kilometers off Cape Cod, Newfoundland with a loss of 129 men. Thresher was found after an extensive search.

Thresher had just undergone an extensive overhaul, and the accident occurred during a diving exercise. The last unclear message obtained from the boat was: 'We have certain difficulties . . . have a positive angle . . . are trying to blow out . . .'; and later sounds were interpreted as a collapse. A court of inquiry blamed the disaster on a failure in the piping system which flooded the vessel. One theory is that failure of a seawater pipe caused a violent stream of pressurized water to hit the nuclear control board, initiating an emergency shutdown of the reactor. Power was lost and Thresher went down.

The inquiry revealed several problems including inadequate stored air pressure for blowing dry ballast tanks for emergency surfacing. Later submarines of the *Permit* class and successive classes were delayed because of safety programme modifications.

The second American nuclear submarine, *Scorpion*, vanished in June 1968 with 99 men aboard. She was found 650 kilometers southwest of the Azores at a depth of 3 100 meters. Scorpion was underway from Gibraltar to Norfolk, Virginia. The best theory involves a torpedo room fire as the cause of the accident. A Naval Inquiry Court later reported that 'the certain cause of the loss of Scorpion cannot be ascertained from any evidence now available'. One month before, Scorpion had collided with a barge during a storm in Naple's harbour in Italy. The submarine was alongside the barge which was used as a buffer between the submarine and another US warship. The barge and the Scorpion's stern came together and then the barge went down. Divers made a partial inspection and reported no damage.

According to a memorandum dated April 26, 1989, by the UK Ministry of Defence on the sinking of Soviet submarines, an unknown type of nuclear submarine sank at Severomorsk on the Kola Peninsula, in 1968. This sinking has not been admitted by the Soviet authorities. Another source (CIA) provided the raw intelligence information that this submarine was overdue from patrol. After two or three days of waiting, a search was initiated. The submarine was found on the bottom of the Kolskiy Zaliv estuary. When the submarine was recovered it was found that all food had been consumed and it was estimated that the submarine had been at that location for 30 days. 90 crewmen died. This submarine is most probably salvaged.

A Soviet nuclear submarine of the *November* class sank in April 1970 about 300 nautical miles north-west of Spain. The cause of this ship wreck is not known. On April 11 the submarine was sighted dead in the water with personnel on deck trying to rig a tow line to two accompanying Soviet ships. By the morning of April 12 US Navy patrol planes only observed two oil slicks on the surface where the submarine had been. The submarine was scuttled, with loss of life, to prevent fire from reaching the nuclear propulsion plant. The accident is believed to be related to a problem in the nuclear propulsion system. Soviet survey vessels patrolled the area for a period of 10 years, presumably to take water samples to check potential radioactive releases and to advise other nations not to interfere.

In May 1983 a Soviet nuclear submarine of the modern *Charlie* class went down with all hands near her home-base at Kamtchatka in the North Pacific. The ship was salvaged in August the same year. According to Japanese sources 90 crewmen lost their lives. The accident was probably due to a mechanical failure unrelated to the nuclear propulsion plant. There was no evidence of radioactive contamination. In a statement June 1989 from the Soviet authorities, a Soviet submarine (the type was not specified) went down in June 1983 'while leaving a bay'. The submarine sank at a depth of 50 meters. 16 men died. The submarine was later salvaged. The two reports probably refer to one and the same event.

Fig. 2 View of a Soviet Yankee class which sank in the North Atlantic 1 000 kilometers north-east of the Bermudas in 1986 after a fire and explosion in one of the port banks of missile tubes.

In October 1986 a Soviet nuclear submarine of the *Yankee* class went down about 1 000 kilometers north-east of the Bermudas in the Atlantic. The submarine was operating submerged when a fire started, followed by an explosion in one of the port banks of missile tubes. This damaged the hull. The 8 000 tonnes SSBN is armed with 16 SS-N-6 missiles. A fire in the two-stage liquid fuel rocket motor would generate considerable heat and smoke. The Soviet authorities refused US offers of help. After two attempts to limp home under its own power, and three days of fire-fighting while the disabled vessel was taken in tow by a Soviet merchant ship, the submarine was ultimately abandoned and sank at a depth of 5 000 meters. Three crewmen died and several were injured.

A dramatic event happened on April 6 1989, 180 km south-west of Bear Island in the Norwegian Sea when a Soviet nuclear submarine of the advanced *Mike* class caught fire and sank at a depth of 1 685 meters. Press reports based on interviews with crew members indicate that a fire started in the aft engine compartment 6 while in submerged operation. A liquid had been observed leaking from a hydraulic system. The compartment was not a reactor area, but contained reduction gear and/or diesel engines. It took 15 minutes to surface. The fire spread to compartments 4 and 5 which housed the reactor cooling pumps and the reactors. A fire then started at a control desk in section 3. All attempts to extinguish the fires were in vain. The automatic reactor safety system was said to be operating and the nuclear power plant was closed down. Several explosions were heard, and the ship was abandoned. 44 crewmen, including the captain, died after an heroic effort to save trapped crew members.

Fig. 3 The Soviet nuclear submarine Mike, the only one of her class, observed in the Norwegian Sea by the Norwegian Air Force before the fire accident which led to the loss of the submarine and the tragic loss of 44 men.

Collisions

Collisions involving nuclear submarines do occur occasionally. In November 1969 the USS *Gato* collided with a Soviet submarine 30–40 kilometers from the inlet to the White Sea. Press reports indicated that neither Gato nor the Soviet submarine was damaged. Weapons were kept ready for self-defence. None of the parties were apparently interested in exploiting the episode politically, since it was kept secret for many years.

In 1973 the US Defence Department reported that a damaged Soviet *Echo II* class submarine was observed south of Cuba with an eight-foot gash in the port bow deck, probably due to a collision with a Soviet cruiser with visible scratches on its hull.

In May 1974 a US nuclear attack submarine *Pintado* collided almost head-on with a Soviet Yankee class nuclear submarine while cruising 200 feet deep in the approaches to the Petropavlovsk naval base on the Kamtchatka Peninsula. The Soviet submarine surfaced immediately. The extent of damage is not known. The Pintado, which was on an intelligence gathering mission in Soviet territorial waters, departed at top speed from the area and was repaired at Guam.

In November 1983 a *Victor* class submarine was involved in a collision with the US *McCloy*, and it has been reported that in March 1984 a Soviet nuclear submarine collided with the US aircraft carrier *Kitty Hawk* in the Japanese Sea.

Rumours have been heard that an Alfa class submarine was moving with a speed of 40 knots when it collided with a whale. The collision was fatal to the whale and a shocking experience to the submarine which apparently sustained serious damage. It is estimated that there are about 70 000 minke whales in the North Atlantic.

Two other collisions call for a smile. In 1983 a US submarine on a cruise near the Japanese coast planned to surface. The captain intended to check his whereabouts. By chance he unhappily pushed the submarine periscope into the bottom of a Japanese fishing boat. This tantalizing situation could be described in a free adaptation of Henrik Ibsen:

Curses from above
and despair from below
met in the same blow

– or vice versa.

The other collision took place in the Straits of Gibraltar in September 1984. A Soviet nuclear submarine of the *Victor I* class tried to slip undetected out of the Mediterranean through the Straits by moving in the noise shadow from a Soviet tanker. This is a well-known procedure to avoid detection by sound-tracking systems. Stratification of water with different salinities and thus different densities probably created internal tidal waves in the sea. This gave the submarine buoyancy an unexpected uplift which resulted in collision with the tanker. The submarine suffered a crushed nose and a dose of humiliation. The double hull structure saved the submarine from a total loss. The submarine was repaired provisionally and was able to return to the home base at the Kola Peninsula.

Fig. 4 After a serious collision with a friendly tanker in the Strait of Gibraltar in 1984, the Soviet submarine Victor I in the Norwegian Sea on her return to the bases at the Kola Peninsula.

The collision of a German submarine (non-nuclear) with a Norwegian oil-rig in the North Sea in 1988 would give cause for amusement as well, if it were not for the inherent risks involved. A major oil-spill could have been the result. If this had been laced with a spread of radioactive substances from a leaky nuclear plant, no one would have smiled.

Fires and explosions

Fires and explosions frequently occur. In the two cases of Yankee in 1986 and Mike in 1989 this led to the submarine sinking. On September 18, 1984 the crew of a Japanese shrimp-trawler noticed that their vessel was being pulled backwards. The trawl was at a depth of 60 meters and had to be cut. Two days later a Japanese aeroplane discovered a Soviet (non-nuclear) submarine of the *Golf II* class in surface position 85 kilometers East of Okinoshima Island in the Japanese Sea. Thick white smoke was escaping from the submarine sail and from the openings covering the missiles. A number of crewmen were observed on deck. Japanese planes offered assistance which was refused. Soviet rescuing vessels accompanied the submarine, which after 50 hours of fire-fighting was observed moving under her own power towards Vladivostok in the Soviet Union.

Golf II class submarines are diesel propelled and in 1984 they were furnished with liquid fuel propelled SSN-5 missiles. One theory is that the fire might have been due to leakages of this fuel. Another way of explaining the accident is that the fire broke out in the struggle of escaping from the trawlers trap. Whatever the real true reason, fires do occur and occasionally with catastrophic consequences.

In August 1980 a Soviet nuclear submarine of the *Echo I* class was observed on fire off Okinawa in the Pacific.

Groundings

Groundings are rarely reported to the public. A notable exception was the *Whiskey on the Rocks* incident at the entrance to the Swedish Naval Base in Karlskrona on October 27, 1981. The non-nuclear propelled Soviet submarine of the *Whiskey* class was on its way home from an exercise in the Southern Baltic. The ship managed to hit Sweden while the Captain claimed that faulty instruments prophesied they were in Polish waters. A closer scrutiny of the local map indicates, however, that local manoeuvering in this case must have been exceptionally adept.

On March 13, 1986 the USS nuclear submarine *Nathaneal Greene* ran aground in the Irish Sea. External damage was done to her ballast tanks and rudder. 'There was no effect on the propulsion, no injuries and no damage to the Poseidon nuclear missiles', according to a US Navy spokesman. After emergency repairs at Holy Loch, Scotland, the submarine returned submerged to the USA. The extent of damage subsequently led to a decision to decommission the vessel, partly in order to satisfy SALT II limitations (ref. 1)

Propulsion plant accidents

There is – and rightly so – an urgent need for a definition of what events deserve the public attention of being termed a nuclear accident. According to one US naval regulation, a nuclear reactor accident is defined as: 'An uncontrolled reactor criticality resulting in damage to the reactor core or an event such as loss of coolant which results in significant release of fission products from the reactor core'. On the basis of such a high-threshold definition, the US Navy proudly testifies to Congress that 'there has never been a reactor accident in the history of the US Naval Nuclear Propulsion Program . . .', and, 'As of the Spring of 1989, the Navy has had over 3 500 reactor-years of operation without a reactor accident'. This sounds indeed impressive, but the statements imply that incidents below this threshold might well have occurred. We will never know whether incidents have happened where the avoidance of damage to the reactor core or avoidance of significant releases of fission products from the core have been due to sheer luck.

The Soviets have not had that luck. Accidents have occurred with their reactor plants. There are several cases on record where their nuclear submarines have been observed at sea with loss of power. In 1961 a submarine, probably of the *Hotel* class, had an accident near the coast of England. Crew members were seriously contaminated when a

Fig. 5 Break-down of the nuclear propulsion plant in a Soviet submarine of the Echo II class in the Norwegian Sea June 26, 1989. Steam from the reactor plant is observed billowing out from the submarine while the crew has gathered on the deck.

cooling pipe broke. The radiation level in the area where the pipe broke was said to be five roentgens per hour. This is a high radiation level, but not dramatically so. A crew member would, if being exposed to this radiation field, have obtained his maximum permissible annual radiation dose in about one hour.

On February 24 1972 a Hotel class submarine was observed on the surface 600 miles north-east of Newfoundland with an apparent nuclear propulsion problem which had resulted in the loss of power. The next day the submarine was observed in the company of five Soviet ships. Offers of assistance were not answered. On March 18 the submarine was moving slowly in the north Atlantic, and on April 5 she reached home waters in the White Sea.

In August 1978 an Echo II class was observed dead in the water near Rockall Bank north of Scotland following loss of power due to a propulsion system casualty. The submarine was towed back to the Soviet Union.

In September 1981 a nuclear submarine operating in the Baltic had an accident. Crew members were reportedly sealed in the reactor compartment and suffered severe irradiation. The submarine was towed back to the Soviet Union.

'Foreign objects' penetrating into Scandinavian fjords

The Soviet Union is being accused of sending submarines into Scandinavian coastal waters. The Karlskrona incident provided ample evidence that this is the case in Sweden. More than 100 incidents have been reported where 'foreign objects' (read: submarines) have been observed – or are believed to have been observed – in Norwegian fjords during the last 10–15 years. A review of the incidents reported for the period 1975–1989 is shown in fig. 6 (ref. 2).

The number of nuclear vessels in international and Norwegian coastal waters is so large that Norwegian authorities and the public are showing an increasing awareness of the potential dangers. The recent (1989) three Soviet nuclear submarine accidents in the Norwegian Sea are a tragic reminder of this.

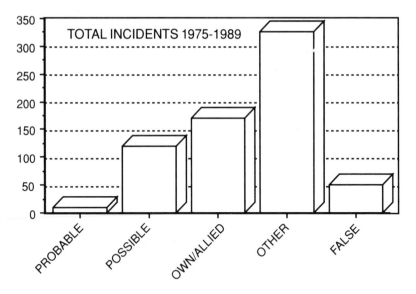

Fig. 6 Submarine-like objects in Norwegian fjords, 1975–1989.

2 Nuclear submarines: How they look and how they are propelled

Access to the type of information needed for safety assessments of nuclear submarines is indeed limited. One has to rely on generic information relating to the design, operation and safety assessments of civilian nuclear power plants, landbased as well as marine plants. To some extent, this might be adequate. Vital information on reactor fuel design and operational properties is, however, lacking. The vulnerability of submarines to shocks from internal explosive charges is a specific feature of submarines with no parallel in civilian nuclear power plants.

To perform an ideal assessment of the potential dangers of sunken nuclear submarines information would be needed concerning:

– general design and construction of nuclear submarines
– types and layouts of the nuclear plants used
– design, strength and function of all protective barriers surrounding the nuclear fuel
– vulnerability of these protective barriers to collisions or accidents, in particular to shocks from the explosive charges stored onboard the submarine (torpedoes and missile propellant fuel)
– design power level of the nuclear plant and operating history of core prior to damage

Two Western civilian nuclear-propelled cargo-ships have been constructed in the USA and the Federal Republic of Germany. Both are now out of operation. Extensive safety reports relating to these ships, containing a wealth of generic information, have been published. The Soviet Union has six nuclear propelled ice-breakers and one nuclear propelled cargo-ship in operation. A limited amount of technical information on these civilian plants has been published. It would be surprising if the nuclear plants of the Soviet nuclear submarines and the nuclear ice-breakers did not have most design features in common.

In 1982 the International Maritime Organization (IMO), London, issued a Code of Safety, written in very general terms, for nuclear merchant ships. The Soviet nuclear propelled cargo-ship has been designed in accordance with the rules of this Code. The Code undoubtedly reflects sound engineering principles and has therefore provided some guidance in the writing of this book.

The submarine

There are three types of nuclear submarines, each with distinct operative tasks. The first category (SSBN) is the submarine carrying ballistic nuclear weapons and the second (SSCN) is equipped with cruise missiles. The third category is the attack submarine (SSN).

This book is not concerned with the submarine weaponry or warfare combat power. Its purpose is to describe the inventory of radioactive materials in the propulsion plant, to describe the various barriers which exist between this inventory and the environment, and what might happen to these barriers under adverse operating conditions for submarines.

Categories of submarines

First a brief description of the three categories of nuclear submarines.

The ballistic missile submarines (SSBN's) are the largest ones. An impressive example is the Soviet *Typhoon* class with a displacement of 25–30 000 tonnes submerged. The Typhoon carries 20 SS-N-20 Sturgeon ballistic missiles fitted with 10 MIRVed nuclear warheads. The yield per warhead is 100 Kt. In addition, there are either 6 or 8 torpedo tubes. A stowage capacity of 40 missiles and torpedoes has been considered possible.

The *Ohio* class nuclear submarines are the largest submarines built in the West. They carry 24 ballistic Trident I C-4 missiles which will be replaced by Trident II C-5 now under development. Each missile carries 8 100kT MIRVed nuclear warheads. All Ohios are deployed in the Pacific.

Fig. 7 View of the USS Ohio class ballistic missile nuclear submarine.

The second category is the cruise missile submarine, the SSGN. The Soviet *Oscar II* is one submarine in this category and is shown in fig. 8. The large beam was necessary to accommodate large-diameter vertical launch tubes for the SS-N-19 Shipwreck cruise-missiles. Not all of the missiles are nuclear tipped. The 6 hatches on each side of the fin are seen in the picture. There are two missile tubes under each hatch.

The old Soviet Echo II class is another submarine carrying cruise-missiles, see fig. 33. They are equipped with 8 launch tubes for the SS-N-12 Sandbox missiles. The launch tubes are flush with the upper corners of the hull casing. They elevate in pairs to an angle of 15 degrees for firing. Indentations in the hull casing abaft the launchers serve to deflect the blast of the missile exhaust away from the hull. The missiles can only be launched when the submarine is in surface position.

The USS *Permit* and the French *Rubis* class are examples of the third category, the nuclear attack submarines, SSNs. Fig. 9 shows a Permit class submarine. The original name-ship of this class, Thresher, was lost with all hands less than two years after her completion in 1961. The Permit class is fitted with four torpedo tubes designed to fire nuclear-tipped missiles against both surface ships and submarines.

The French attack submarine Rubis is the smallest nuclear submarine ever built. A layout of her nuclear propulsion plant is presented in fig. 27.

Fig. 8 View of the Soviet Oscar II class cruise-missile nuclear submarine.

Fig. 9 View of the USS Permit class attack nuclear submarine.

Nuclear versus diesel-electric propulsion

A diesel-driven conventional submarine stores energy in batteries which then propel the submarine with electric motors. The energy storage capacity of batteries is small. A submarine can therefore only operate immersed for a limited time before the batteries need to be charged. The diesel engine needs oxygen and the submarine will have to surface, or, alternatively, suck air through a snorkel. This limitation is inherent with conventional submarines. Nuclear propulsion plants do not require oxygen; on the contrary, they can actually produce oxygen from water by electrolysis. The energy necessary for this process is in abundant supply from the nuclear power plant.

Operational features of nuclear submarines

The most striking difference between conventional and nuclear submarines is the increased endurance and speed of the latter. Nuclear submarines have demonstrated their ability to cruise submerged around the globe without surfacing. The first crossing of the North Polar Basin under the ice was made by USN *Nautilus* in 1958 and is routine technology today.

Another remarkable feature of the nuclear submarine is that (in the Western submarines) the propulsion plant only needs refuelling every 8–10 years, thanks to a striking development in fuel element technology. Refitting the core is a major process taking 12 to 18 months. Part of this time is probably needed to let the core cool down before removal.

Modern submarines are designed for operating in the Arctic. The fins used for manouvering during diving operations can be turned vertically to reduce resistance while surfacing through the ice. Soviet submarines are believed to have reinforced sails for this reason. The higher freeboards which are characteristic of Soviet submarines are probably also due to their being better adapted to operating in the Arctic.

High speed requires high capacity propulsion plants, and nuclear energy has turned out to be ideal for this purpose. Nuclear submarines are able to sustain high speeds submerged for periods limited only by crew endurance.

Submarine hull construction

The submarine hull is one of the barriers – the ultimate one – between the radioactive fission products in the nuclear plant and the environment. There are four main types of hull construction: single hulls, double hulls, saddle tank and multiple hulls. Single-hull designs are most frequently used by the Western fleets, while Soviet designers seem to prefer double hulls. Single-hull submarines have their main ballast tanks either mounted externally at each end of the pressure hull or within the hull itself. Saddle-tank designs use ballast tanks mounted externally as streamlined additions to the pressure hull. In double-hull designs an outer hull surrounds the pressure hull. The space between them is used for ballast tanks and external fuel storage.

Improved metallurgical properties of plating materials, more sophisticated welding and welding control techniques and better techniques for permissive pressure loads on the hull have created unique opportunities to design submarines with greater diving depths and increased speeds. Under normal operating conditions modern hull designs are expected to provide larger safety margins in the event of an accident. There are, however, many nuclear submarine classes in operation which were constructed in the early 1960s. A number of these have experienced severe accidents and mishaps. Five rest on the seabed (a sixth is a very modern submarine). The hulls of the two most recently sunken Soviet submarines were destroyed from the inside, apparently due to violent explosions or fires.

There are close connections between maximum diving depth, capacity of the propulsion plant necessary for a specified maximum speed and material specifications for the pressure hull. The crucial parameter combining these requirements is 'volume weight', measured in tons per cubic meter.

When submerged, the submarine is in neutral buoyancy, i.e. the total weight of the submarine equals the weight of the water it displaces. The total weight consists of the pressure hull, possibly an outer hull as well, the main propulsion machinery, auxiliary machinery, weapons, trimming ballasts etc. If the weight of any of them is increased, the weight of something else has to be reduced to preserve neutral buoyancy. The interplay between these parameters is presented in a graph, fig. 10 (ref. 4).

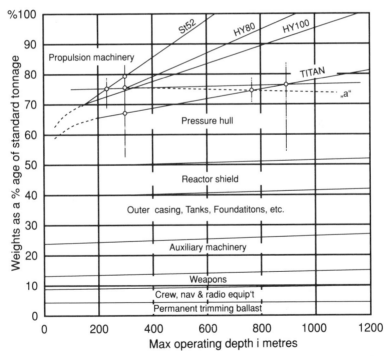

Fig 10 Interplay between relative weights of major components, construction material quality of the pressure hull and diving depths of submarines.

In this graph the weights are given as percentages of standard tonnage against maximum diving depths in meters. Half of a submarine's total weight is composed of components which are quite insensitive to whether the submarine is designed for large or small diving depths. The other half is divided between the hull(s) and the propulsion machinery. The graph illustrates the influence of various H(igh) Y(ield) steels, HY80 (the number gives the yield stress in pounds per square inch) and HY100 or St52, on what weight is available for the propulsion plant. For small operating depths the choice of steel quality does not matter very much. At diving depths of 400–600 meters the effect is more apparent. Use of titanium, however, has a substantial influence.

In the 1960s a Norwegian *Orion* surveillance aircraft discovered that a new Soviet submarine did not respond with the usual magnetic signature originating from ships. This discovery revealed that the new submarine, later labelled *Alfa*, had a non-magnetic structural material in its hull. It was pretty obvious that this material could not be anything but titanium.

Titanium has several properties which make it especially attractive. It has 43 percent greater tensile strength than HY80 steel, but its weight is only 58 percent of that of steel. Titanium is very resistant to corrosion. It can be used for pipes in cooling systems and heat exchangers, and – of particular importance for submarine hulls – it is virtually non-magnetic. There are drawbacks as well, though; for one thing, it is less elastic than steel. This can be remedied by proper alloying with other elements, for instance aluminium or manganese. Furthermore, it creeps under heavy loads. Creep is a slow plastic deformation which does not return to the original state when the load is removed. It is therefore necessary to keep account of the total period under strain. The ultimate life of a titanium pressure hull might depend on the number of stress cycles experienced in operation. Titanium is also difficult to weld and it is very expensive, (ref. 4).

The Soviets have apparently carried out outstanding development work on titanium technology to permit them to introduce this material in submarines on such a large scale.

A demand for greater diving depth means that the hull plating (and structure) must be heavier. If this is achieved at the expense of the weight of the propulsion machinery, the submarine speed has to be reduced. There are two ways to circumvent this problem: either to choose a lighter plating material while still providing the necessary strength to sustain a specified diving depth, or to design a power propulsion source with higher specific power. The Soviets have done both.

The Alfa class submarine has probably only one hull. A tentative hull shape is shown in fig. 11.

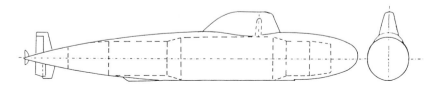

Fig. 11 Tentative hull shape of the Soviet Alfa class submarine.

If the hull had been constructed for a diving depth of 300 meters using HY80 steel, the hull would have weighed 875 tons, (ref. 4). This corresponds to 25 percent of the submarine's dry-weight. With a titanium line inserted in the graph it is apparent that, if titanium is used instead of HY80 steel, the diving depth would be 900 meters, with St50 steel, 230 meters and with HY100, 335 meters. At a diving depth of 300 meters the relative available weight for the main engines is 24.5 percent for HY80 and 33 percent for titanium, (ref. 4). (The US Navy is planning to use HY130 in their new SSN *Seawolf* now under construction). Use of titanium will therefore, at unchanged diving depths, permit a heavier propulsion plant, or more power. The Soviets have used titanium in their freedom of design in order to increase diving depth. In addition, another type of propulsion plant using a liquid-metal coolant which provides higher specific power, i.e. more megawatts per unit weight, has permitted higher speed.

Modern submarines will most probably maximize the use of lightweight materials like fibreglass and composite materials of various types for internal structures. This was the case with the Soviet Mike submarine and could at least in part explain the rapid development of the fire which led to the sinking of the submarine. The materials offered apparently reduced resistance to outbreak of fires.

The nuclear 'work-horse': The pressurized-water reactor propulsion plant (PWR)

The PWR consists of a primary system containing a nuclear fuel core, control rod systems, pressure tank, pressurizer and steam-generators with necessary pumps, and a secondary system comprising steam turbines, steam condenser and auxiliary systems. A mechanical clutch and gear system transfers the power to the propeller shaft. A layout of a typical PWR propulsion plant is shown in fig. 12. How does it work?

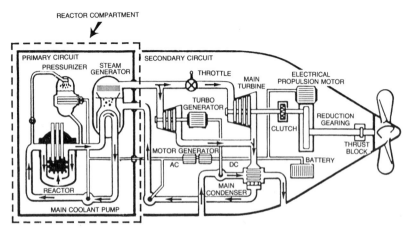

Fig. 12 Layout of a dispersed PWR nuclear propulsion plant showing the reactor compartment containing the reactor primary circuit, and the reactor secondary circuit with turbines, condensor, reduction gear and auxiliary equipment.

The reactor's primary system

The neutron chain reaction leads under controlled conditions to fissions of uranium-235 nuclei in such a large number per second that the nuclear fuel in the reactor core heats up. The temperature within the fuel can be extremely high, more than 1 000 °C. The surface of the fuel elements is cooled by water which is prevented from boiling by an external pressurizer. The coolant water is heated up and the heat is delivered to an external steam generator which transfers the heat from the primary to the secondary reactor system.

Explanatory frame: The chain reaction

One neutron is sufficient to provoke a fission of a uranium-235 or plutonium-239 nucleus. During the fission of this nucleus 2 to 3 new neutrons are emitted (some fissions give 2 neutrons, others 3, on the average 2.43). These neutrons can in principle be absorbed by another 'fissile' isotope (uranium-235) which might then fission, releasing more neutrons and so on. This process is labelled a 'chain process'. The chain process is the fundamental basis of all nuclear weapons and nuclear reactors, either civilian or military. The very first neutron starting the process usually comes from a 'neutron source'.

There are two ways of designing the primary system: either dispersed as in fig. 12, or integrated, fig. 14. This distinction is of some importance when considering the safety characteristics of the two designs.

Primary system designs can either be dispersed –
The main feature of a dispersed primary design (loop design) is that the steam transformer, pressurizer and primary pumps are separated by pipes. Another example of a dispersed primary system design is the one used by the Soviet cargo lighter carrier, launched in 1987, see fig. 30. It is reported that this design has undergone practically no change compared to the earlier nuclear plants of the ice-breakers *Lenin* and *Arktika*. Keeping in mind the importance and advantages of series production of the major components, one may therefore speculate that this design reflects solutions adopted in Soviet submarine design as well. The primary system has a pressure tank containing the fuel core, and a number of steam generators with related primary pumps connected to the pressure tank by short pipes. The pressure tank is fixed to the upper cover of another tank containing iron plates and water for shielding purposes. The supporting structure of this tank also accommodates pressurizers, primary filters and a filter condenser.

Compared to the Arktika plant, the power plant of the icebreaker/cargo-ship includes changes in the design of biological shielding, new layout arrangements for safety systems, and new principles for forming the protective barriers of the nuclear plant. This is a result of the Soviet Union fulfilling the requirements of the International Maritime

Organization (IMO) Code of Safety for the design of civilian nuclear cargo ships.

Submarine reactor pressure vessels are most probably made of mild steel with an internal cladding of stainless steel. This is the practice adopted in the corresponding civilian power plants. The design, however, might deviate. A submarine plant has to be designed to strict specifications in order to absorb shocks from exploding warheads. The nature of these specifications is not known. A view of the design of a typical reactor plant's pressure vessel is given in fig. 13. The pressure

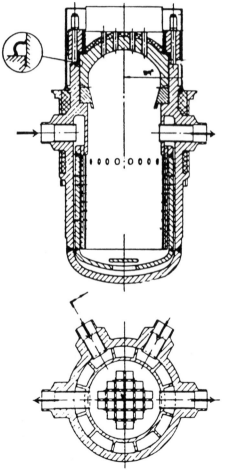

Fig. 13 The pressure vessel and core configuration of the US S5W reactor propulsion plant.

vessel consists of a lower part containing the reactor core, supporting arrangements for the core and a thermal shield composed of several annular iron-plates to reduce the direct neutron and gamma radiation from the core. An upper part which is removable provides access to the interior for fuel replacement.

– or they can be integrated

The weight and space requirements of the nuclear plant are necessarily of prime concern for the designer. Since the biological shielding (see below) surrounding the reactor will be a heavy lump, any compaction of the primary system will in turn, hopefully, compact the shielding, as well as reducing its weight. One way to achieve this is to integrate the steam generator with pumps and the pressurizer within the pressure tank, see fig. 14.

The NS *Otto Hahn* has this type of integrated primary reactor system. The primary water flows through the fuel elements in direct contact with the fuel pins and is heated up to 278 °C. The water flows further through the upper plenum into the steam generator which is situated in the circular space between the pressure vessel wall and the plenum. In this steam generator the primary water is cooled to 267 °C when it leaves the steam generator. There are three stalk-mounted primary circulation pumps which pump the water back into the fuel elements.

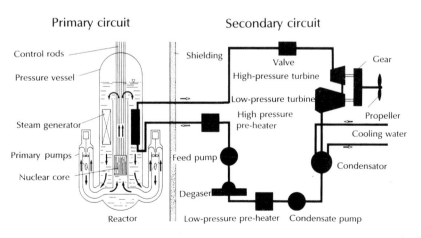

Fig. 14 Layout of the integrated primary reactor system of NS Otto Hahn.

The integrated designs proposed in the earlier days of civilian nuclear propulsion had to be rejected, primarily because of a risk of sea
water leaking into the primary system. This could in turn lead to severe
corrosion problems if filters and water purification systems did not
function properly. Development work in the nuclear power industry
has solved this problem. It is reported that the reactor in the French
submarine Rubis has an integrated primary system.

The Soviet Mike class submarine which sank tragically in the North
Atlantic in April 1989 is believed to have had an advanced type of propulsion plant. In fact, it was assumed to be a liquid-metal cooled plant
similar to the one in the Alfa class. The Soviets, questioned by the
Norwegian authorities about the type of reactor plant, surprisingly re-
sponded that, contrary to general belief, Mike was equipped with a
PWR plant. If Mike is still considered to have an advanced, experimental propulsion plant, one might speculate that the novelty of the
plant was an integrated primary system.

The biological shielding
The direct neutron and gamma radiation field from the reactor core
under operation is tremendous. A biological shield is necessary to protect the crew and the environment. There is a high premium on saving
space and weight in a submarine. Water (or polyeten) is a suitable medium for shielding against neutrons, and iron and lead readily absorb
gamma-rays. A tentative solution for a biological shielding is shown in
fig. 15.

The biological shielding protects the environment from the direct
gamma radiation from the core, also when the submarine rests on the
seabed. However, this shielding does not act as a barrier against the release of fission products that may be released later on from the reactor
core.

The reactor's secondary system
The secondary system of the reactor consists of turbines, the main condenser, feed-water systems, auxiliary systems, clutch and gear for connection to the propeller shaft and emergency core cooling systems. Alternatively, clutch and gear systems can be replaced by a turbo-electric
system. Turbo generators provide electric power to operate an electric
engine turning the propeller shaft. The French Rubis has this kind of
turbo-electric system.

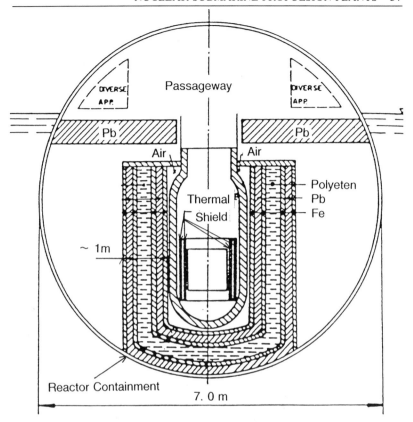

Fig. 15 The biological shielding consists of interspersed layers of water, iron and lead. High energy neutrons from the core are slowed down in the water and subsequently absorbed in the iron and lead.

Whereas the primary systems of submarine and ice-breaker nuclear plants may have very much in common, their secondary systems may deviate in thermal design. Every kilogram of weight introduced in a submarine's propulsion plant is at the expense of added weaponry or increased pressure hull thickness (diving capability).

Exhaust pressure and temperature at the condenser determine the necessary surface area and hence the weight and volume of the condenser for a given power level. Exhaust pressures below 3–4 psia are impractical because then the condenser gets too big. This is in contrast to ice-breaker propulsion plants where in Arktika an exhaust pressure of 1 psia is used. This condenser type requires almost three times the condensing surface compared with one which operates at 3 psia, for the same mass flow.

Plant parameters of Soviet submarine secondary systems can deviate from the corresponding cargo lighter carrier version. The 135-megawatt primary system of the latter delivers steam to the turbines at a temperature of 285 °C with a thermal efficiency of about 23 percent.

The electric power system of the cargo vessel includes primary, reserve and emergency supplies of power. Nuclear submarines, obviously, have similar systems. The main electric power plant consists of three turbo generators with a capacity of 2 megawatts each containing mounted condensers with their own circulation and condensate pumps.

The nuclear heart of the work-horse: The fuel core

The nuclear fuel core is the very heart of the propulsion plant. Preserving the integrity of the fuel under any adverse operational or combat situation is a fundamental condition for continued operability of the submarine. Hardly any facts are released to the public about submarine fuel designs. Because of its fundamental importance for the submarine as a weapon carrier this subject is obviously highly sensitive.

On the other hand, the fuel is the very source of radioactive fission products. The fundamental problem is then: under what conditions may accidental release occur? It should be pointed out that all the basic processes which govern the production, composition, storage and containment of fission products in the fuel structure, measures for protection of the fuel and risk potential for inadvertent releases, are familiar from the civilian nuclear industry. These processes are well documented. Secrecy is maintained only for commercial reasons. However, experience from the civilian nuclear industry is most likely not directly transferable to submarine fuel. The two types of fuel might not only differ in the choice of mechanical design, but material specifications and production technologies probably do not overlap.

The following is therefore an application of the general strategy previously outlined of 'searching under the nearest street-light where the light is better'!

Choice of nuclear fuel

US submarines today use uranium with an enrichment in the isotope U-235 of 97.3 percent, (ref. 5). This is even higher than weapon-grade uranium (93 percent). Why this high enrichment? According to information given by the Soviet authorities in the wake of the Mike accident in April 1989, the Soviet submarines are using 'modestly enriched' uranium. Soviet data on Mike can be interpreted to imply an enrichment in the range of 10 percent. In contrast, civilian nuclear power plants and civilian propulsion plants – NS Otto Hahn, NS Savannah and the Soviet ice-breakers – are using uranium fuel enriched to the range of 4–6 percent. Furthermore, is plutonium being used as a submarine fuel? If not, why?

The enrichment level per se is not the issue. However, through appropriate choice of enrichment level it is possible to design a core with a long operative life. Modern US submarine cores can sustain operation 15 years before refuelling becomes necessary. This means that the submarine will need refuelling just once in its lifetime, an obvious operative advantage. It will be fruitful to view enrichment in the context of other design parameters like operational temperature limits and metallurgical constraints on the choice of construction materials.

Illustrative examples of the interplay between design parameters have been taken from:

– civilian nuclear power plant fuels
– civilian propulsion plant fuels
– fuel used in research and material testing reactors

By combining information on fuel from these plants, one can tentatively deduce which requirements submarine fuel will have to fulfil in order to achieve the submarine's operative goals.

Civilian nuclear power plant fuels
A primary source of information on fuel technology which might shed some ('street'–) light on the submarine fuel is the civilian nuclear power plant fuel. Uranium-235 is an excellent fuel material and is in abundant supply. The fuel element production technology is well developed. Civilian fuel technology has direct relevance for submarine fuel with low enrichments only. However, in order to illustrate operational factors which influence the binding or release of fission products from damaged fuel elements, aspects of this technology will be described. It is less certain to which extent these aspects are similar or different from the corresponding ones in submarine fuel.

The fuel pin shown in fig. 16 is typical for a civilian power reactor.

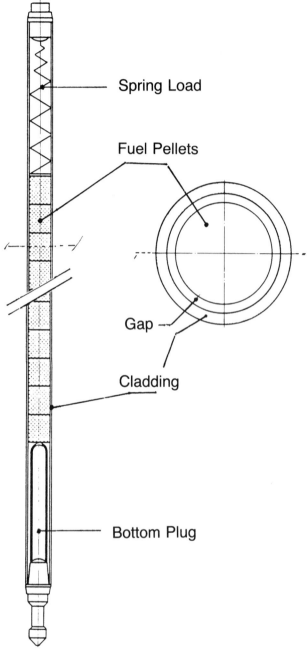

Fig. 16 A civilian nuclear fuel pin with fuel pellets, fuel gap and cladding.

The characteristic pin diameter is 1/2 inch (12 mm). The length may be 13ft (3.9 m). A civilian power station might have 45 000 of these pins sub-divided into 190 fuel elements of 236 pins each.

The fuel 'meat' consists of uranium oxide pellets which are stacked inside the cladding. The pellet column has no structural strength of its own. The cladding takes the full mechanical load imposed by the coolant flow. A full charge weighs approximately 100 tonnes and has a lifetime of 3 years (each year 1/3 of the core is replaced).

Civilian propulsion-reactor core designs

A second source of information is the civilian propulsion-reactor fuel technology. Two Western civilian nuclear cargo ships, NS Savannah and NS Otto Hahn, have fuel designs which are well documented. All civilian nuclear ship designs have in common that their core designs are miniature versions of their landbased counterparts. Their fuel could have been manufactured in the same plant which produces fuel for the civilian nuclear power stations.

A short description is given below of a proposal for an advanced fuel charge design in the German cargo ship project *NCS 80*, see fig. 17. It includes experience acquired from several years of successful operation of NS Otto Hahn, (ref. 6).

Each fuel pin contains uranium oxide enriched to 3–4 percent, encapsulated in a zirconium alloy cladding. The fuel pin has a length of 2.29 meters. The part of the pin containing uranium – or 'active length' – is 1.75 meters. Accordingly, the total active fuelpin length is 22 x 365 x 1.75 meters = 14 052 meters. This length is the source of 220 megawatts of thermal power which corresponds to an average 'linear heat load' of 156 watts per centimeter active fuel length.

The important figure is, however, not the average value, but the peak value. One has to take into account that depending on their placing in the core, some fuel pins, or parts of them, yield more power than others (which again means, of course, that other pins yield less than the average). Peak load could be as much as 3.5 times higher than the average. In this case, peak design value for the linear heat load is about 156 x 3.5 = 546 watts/cm.

No part of the fuel at peak load can be permitted to get so hot that it melts at the centreline. The melting point gives, with a safe margin, a design limit. For a given linear heat load, the centreline temperature

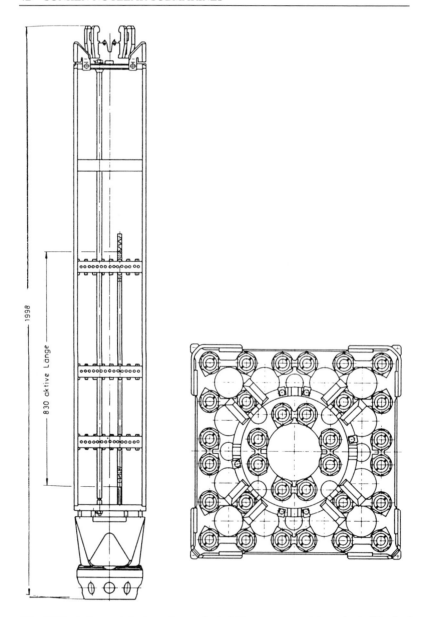

Fig. 17 Fuel element design of a projected German propulsion plant. The fuel charge consists of 24 square 'fuel elements' containing 21x21 lattice positions. Of these positions, 365 are occupied by fuel pins, 44 positions are used for 'control rod pins' and 28 positions contain 'burnable poison' pins which will be described later. This fuel charge contains 8.5 tonnes of uranium-oxide.

turns out to be independent of fuel pin diameter. The diameter, however, has another important limitation.

The heat released inside the fuel pin flows out of the pin through its surface. For any coolant there is an upper limit to the heat load (measured in watts per square centimeter of fuel surface) which can be transferred from fuel to coolant without destroying the cladding material through overheating. Once the coolant (say, water under pressure) and cladding material (stainless steel or zirconium alloy) is chosen, the upper permissible heat load value is fixed. In order to keep the thermal load below the maximum limit allowed, the total surface of the fuel elements must be calculated and this figure determines the fuel pin diameter. If the total thermal load is expected to exceed the limit for any of the pins, more pins must be added in order to even out the load.

It is an important fact that during the chain reaction where uranium isotopes are destroyed, the fuel changes its composition and its mechanical structure. Fission products seep into pores in the fuel structure. One consequence is that the fuel melting point is lowered when the fuel 'burn-up' increases. Another is that the gap between the fuel

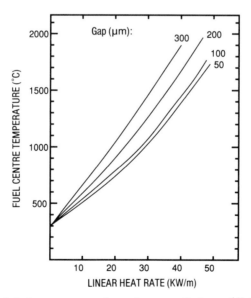

Fig. 18 Central fuel temperature dependence on fuel gap (distance between cladding and fuel) and linear heat. It is seen that the fuel centre temperature is sensitive to the gap size.

and cladding will shrink when the fuel cracks and swells. The release of fission products from the fuel 'meat' into the gap between the fuel proper and the cladding increases as the fuel's temperature rises. All these relationships must be taken into account when designing a fuel charge. Some of them are demonstrated in fig. 18 (ref. 7).

The design parameters determine what fraction of the fission products will be bound to the fuel if the fuel cladding should overheat and rupture. Temperature is the 'driving force' expelling fission products from the fuel pins. The trouble is that although the relationship between these parameters is reasonably well understood for fuel from the civilian nuclear power industry, the information is probably not directly transferable to the evaluation of submarine fuel. One reason for this is that civilian reactor fuel usually is uranium oxide, whereas submarine fuel presumably has a completely different composition.

Fuel designs used in research reactors

The third ('street-light') source of information is fuel designs being used in research and material testing reactors. The purpose of a research reactor is to provide as many excess neutrons as possible for the benefit of the research objectives of the reactor. These objectives are in the fields of material testing, radioactive isotope production for industrial and medical purposes, neutron-activation analysis and in fundamental research using beams of neutrons from the reactor. The number of excess neutrons is directly proportional to the reactor power level (measured in megawatts). These objectives can best be fulfilled by designing a core with a very high power density (kilowatts per liter), a condition which is satisfied if the core is made very small.

Cores with a high power density will inevitably face the heat transfer problem. The most practical solution is to use flat fuel plates instead of fuel pins. A typical configuration is shown in fig. 19. The fuel 'meat' could be shaped as metallic foils inside the cladding, but now another technology has evolved. Uranium fuel, highly enriched in the isotope uranium-235, is dispersed in some other material, called a matrix material, and clad with a third material, usually stainless steel, to make up a fuel plate. The dispersion technology provides fuel 'meat' with a sufficient surface area through which the heat released by the fissions can be transported out of the fuel plate.

Dispersion-type fuel is made by mixing two sorts of powder: one containing uranium and another powder consisting of matrix material.

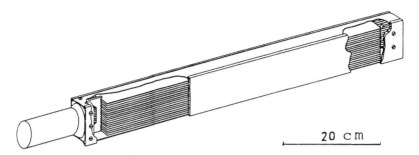

Fig 19 Flat plate fuel design believed to be typical for western submarines.

The uranium powder can be uranium-oxide UO_2, uranium-aluminides UAlx, uranium silicides U_3Si or U_3Si_2 or even U_6Fe. The important consideration is to obtain a high density of the fuel powder (which implies that the uranium content will be high). The matrix powder in research reactor fuel is mainly alumina. Silicides should have advantages too. There is a limitation to how much uranium powder can be introduced into the mixture. (Therefore the high enrichment.) The volume percentage limit seems to be around 44 percent.

A key parameter in the design of high performance fuel elements is the density of the U-235 in the fuel, measured in grams/cm³. In the early days of nuclear age under the American *Atoms for Peace* programme, the US Government strongly advocated that fuel for research reactors should have enrichments not exceeding 20 percent. Since the US Government was the only supplier of enriched uranium this was easily adhered to.

Scientists complained that the reactors needed to be redesigned to provide stronger neutron beams. This implied higher power levels and smaller cores which could not be accomplished without increasing the enrichment to 90–93 percent, i.e. uranium-235 of weapon-grade quality. This was by and large accepted.

In the 1970s concern was again expressed that fuel containing weapon-grade uranium could be diverted to the production of nuclear weapons. Due to pressure from the US Government, research reactor fuel was redesigned by the nuclear power states to contain not more than 20 percent uranium-235 as before. Lowering the enrichment from 93 to 20 percent meant that each fuel element had to contain about 5 times more uranium (of the lower enrichment) in order to retain the same number of uranium-235 isotopes in the element. As long as low-power research reactors were permitted to use 93 percent enriched fuel, low-density fuel containing 1–2 grams total uranium per cubic centimetre was sufficient. The new requirement spurred development of more densely packed fuel similar to the challenge the submarine designers had faced, albeit for a different reason.

Submarine reactor core designs

It is generally believed that submarine fuel is a dispersion-type fuel similar to that used in research reactors. Some of the problems facing the manufacturers of densely packed research reactor fuel must therefore have had their parallels in the production of submarine fuel, and been solved. Nothing is officially known of submarine nuclear fuel designs, production technology and operational data. The technology is probably quite unique. Information is needed in order to:

– assess the maximum possible content of fission products in the core
– assess the ability the fuel has to bind these products to the fuel matrix
  under various accident conditions
– assess the burn-up of the fuel and the lifetime of the core

The actual content of fission products in the core during an accident is determined by the mileage performed according to the submarine logbook, or more specifically, according to the total number of megawatt-days of energy released in the core, adjusted for decay up to the moment the reactor stops. The adjustment will give the composition of the fission products at that moment, i.e. which isotopes are present in which quantities.

This information will probably never be released after an accident. On the other hand, for submarines which sink at large ocean depths, it suffices to know the contents of isotopes with relatively long halflives. Then the dependence on the logbook is not so critical (the number of megawatt-days will suffice), and isotopes with shorter halflives will have died out before any appreciable damage is done. If the submarine has been grounded in shallow coastal waters, all radioactive isotopes are of concern, including those with short halflives.

A US submarine reactor core is reported to contain, on average, 200 kilograms of 97.3 percent enriched uranium-235 (the rest being 2.7 percent uranium-238), (ref. 5). At the time of refuelling, the uranium content has been reduced to 47 kg of 78 percent enriched uranium. The enrichment degradation is due to partial conversion of uranium-235 to uranium-236 by absorption of neutrons not resulting in fissions. This conversion does not contribute to the chain process. A fuel consumption of 153 kg uranium corresponds to an energy release of 1.46×10^5 megawatt-days, assuming that the burning of 1.05 grams of uranium-235 corresponds to a release of 1 megawatt-day of thermal energy. Accordingly, a submarine with a reactor plant operating at a thermal power level of 100 megawatts will be able to cruise at full power for 1 460 days. Refuelling schedules of about 10 years seem reasonable. 100 megawatts thermal power corresponds to about 22 megawatts or 30 000 shaft horsepower to the propeller, assuming an overall thermal efficiency of the nuclear plant of 22 percent, which is probably on the high side. 'Hotel' and equipment load (all other uses of electric power) is not taken into account.

A fuel charge of 200 kg uranium-235 is probably an average core size. This figure has been arrived at by intercomparing published US data on the total processing of enriched uranium and the number of cores produced and replaced in the submarines, (ref. 5). Larger as well as smaller charges are possible. An average submarine charge should be compared with a fuel charge containing no more than 12 kilograms in a research reactor also using highly enriched uranium-235 as fuel. In these reactors the life-time of the core (the time it takes before the core has to be removed and replaced by a fresh core) is measured in weeks. It is therefore obvious that the submarine fuel cores must have very sophisticated designs allowing safe control of the tremendous built-in 'reactivity' of the core. Reactivity is a measure of the ability of the core to sustain a chain-reacting process.

Changes in reactivity are used to control and vary the reactor power level. The point to be made is that the surplus of fuel necessary to provide a long life for the core before refuelling has to be counterbalanced by a mechanism of *burnable poison* which ensures that the powerful reactor core is manageable. The poison binds reactivity and releases it at about the same pace as uranium is burned. This will be described in more detail below.

The matrix containing the fuel substance proper must be able to stand a substantial physical stress over a long time. Each fissioned fuel atom creates two new elemental atoms, which require space within the matrix. The fuel will ultimately swell and deform. The ultimate 'life' of the fuel in the core and accordingly the length of time between refuellings is determined by how much of the uranium content can be fissioned (burned up) before the fuel pins swell and develop cracks.

The choice of enrichment is a more open question. US submarines reportedly use 97.3 percent enrichment, (ref. 5). Lower enrichments are, however, fully possible. The earlier American submarine cores used 18–20 percent and later on 40 percent. The percentage might depend on the metallurgical absorption properties of the matrix material for fission products. The fact that 97.3 percent enrichment is used and not the abundant weapon-grade 93 percent indicates that the volume fraction of fuel mixed into the dispersant has been stretched to its limit.

According to official information from the Soviet Government, Soviet submarines use 'modestly enriched fuel', which may be interpreted as 30–50 percent uranium-235, or even lower. If so, Soviet submarine fuels will most probably have a much shorter operative life-time. Icebreakers, however, use 90 percent enriched fuel.

It is important to know about the properties of the matrix material because it is this matrix that will contain the radioactive fission products. The binding ability of the matrix acts as a very first barrier against leakage to the environment in case of a malfunction or an accident.

Submarine fuel element designs

Based on the above description of civilian propulsion reactor and research and material-testing reactor core designs, a tentative design of a submarine fuel element has to respond to military requirements by:

– being exceedingly reliable in operation
– being compact
– having a thermal design with safe margins to operative limits
– having efficient thermal cycling properties
– permitting high fuel *burn-ups*
– containing extensive 'burnable poison' (see below)

The overall requirement that the fuel design should be exceedingly reliable in operation is pretty obvious. Large margins to operational limits would be one way of ensuring this. The submarines are certainly not testbeds for developing new fuel designs. The development work must be performed in material test reactors, which all nuclear power states have. The US Navy has a 250-megawatt Advanced Testing Reactor (ATR) in Idaho exclusively used for the development and testing of submarine fuel. The Soviets have the added opportunity of using their ice-breakers as test beds. The chugging of the ice-breaker when fighting the ice surely should be of immense value for testing the integrity of the fuel in simulated combat situations. An attractive feature is that the reactor core in an ice-breaker is much more accessible than a submarine core. It is therefore easier to cope with the problems arising with fuel element rupture.

The fuel element must be as shock-proof as possible. In the civilian low-enriched uranium oxide fuel, the cladding is the only structural, load-carrying element. The British have abandoned this type of fuel element in their submarines. The fuel matrix should contribute to fuel stiffness and structural strength.

A submarine power plant deviates significantly in its operating behaviour from a civilian nuclear power plant in one important aspect. The submarine plant must be able to change power level frequently and very fast. The ability to sustain power cycling is therefore essential. A civilian power plant in base load condition can afford to change its power level very slowly during start-up and shut-down. A rate of 3 percent per hour is not unusual (Krummel in FRD). Others (Biblis, also in FRD) quote 0.2 percent per second.

Current civilian fuel technology is able to cope with the necessary power level changes. Propulsion plants, civilian or military, have to respond much faster. For the civilian NS Otto Hahn permissible power level changes are quoted at 4 percent per second. It turned out that under normal operation an average load change of 1 percent per second was sufficient. This is most likely not adequate for submarine fuels. Extensive power cycling of fuel in the test beds will demonstrate whether a design is acceptable or not.

The key to a long refueling period: 'Burnable poison'

How can nuclear submarines operate for 10–15 years between refuelings? Ordinary civilian nuclear power stations of the PWR type change fuel once a year. One third of the fuel charge is then replaced with fresh fuel elements. This means that a full charge lasts about three years. Part of the answer might be that the annual operating time at sea is less than the 70–80 percent operating time of a land-based power station. In addition, the submarine will probably operate at a cruising speed which is much lower than the maximum.

There is an obvious reason why submarine fuel must last as long as possible before replacement. The refuelling operation is a major undertaking in submarines. Although refuelling in civilian power plants certainly is a comprehensive process, they are well equipped for it: the reactor pressure vessel has to be opened and the top lid removed, then the fuel elements are pulled into heavily shielded coffins which are removed by large overhead cranes. This equipment presumes easy access to the reactor interior.

Conditions are quite different in a submarine. Space is precious. There is no room for lifting the highly radioactive fuel elements into the shielded coffin, and there are no overhead cranes to transport the coffins out of the submarine. In fact, the submarine has to be opened by removing a large part of the hull(s) just above the reactor(s). This is a major operation, taking over a year. It is therefore understandable that high priority has been given to the development of fuel which has a long lifetime (has a high fuel *burn-up*). How can this objective be reached?

A fundamental condition for designing such a fuel is that the fuel substance, from a metallurgical point of view, will tolerate the metallurgical stress imposed. Fuel development for civilian power stations over the past decade has succeeded in increasing the burn-up from about 30 000 to about 45 000 megawatt-days per tonne at present. Equivalent numbers for submarine fuel are not known. Suppose that the metallurgy is not a limiting factor. What other conditions have to be fulfilled to achieve high burn-ups?

One way is to put more fuel into the reactor, but this is not a straightforward process. If the amount of fuel is increased above a certain minimum, the so-called 'critical mass', the chain reaction will start. Control can easily be restored by inserting neutron absorbers into the core. These absorbers are known as control rods.

The control rods are usually made of strongly neutron-absorbing materials like silver-indium-cadmium alloys and are in the form of bundles of movable 'pencils' penetrating into the core from above. Some of the control rods are used for regulating the power level. As fuel is burned, the need for absorbing rods is reduced and some rods are pulled out of the core. The demand for high burn-up in densely packed uranium cores is, however, much larger than can be accommodated by movable control rods. A system with fixed mounted rods containing strongly neutron-absorbing isotopes is installed. They bind reactivity and are slowly consumed as they absorb neutrons. When the highly absorbent isotopes are depleted, reactivity is slowly released. This is called the *burnable poison* technique.

The burnable poison system operates in such a way that whenever a reactor designer adds an amount of uranium to the core to increase its life-time, he must also add a corresponding amount of burnable poison to keep the chain process under control.

The term *poison* in this connection relates to the arresting influence the poison has on the neutron chain process. It is technical 'slang' and no poison in the usual sense of the word is involved. The element boron has been used extensively for burnable poison in civilian plants, but now gadolineum has been found to have better characteristics. Civilian fuel is mixed with some gadolineum in oxide form or as a gadolineum-aluminate. There are two isotopes in gadolineum, Gd-155 and Gd-157, which readily absorb neutrons. These isotopes will slowly be depleted to the isotopes Gd-156 and Gd-158 which are harmless to the chain reaction. The 'new' gadolineum will then no longer be a burnable poison. The original gadolineum has been transformed to the new variety of gadolineum, with a different isotopic composition.

The point now is that while the burnable poison has continuously tapped the potent chain reaction process of excess neutrons which otherwise would have rendered the control of the chain process difficult, fuel has been burned leading to the production of fewer neutrons. There is a delicate balance between the burn-ups of fuel and of burnable poison. If the fuel burns up faster than the poison, the chain reaction will suffer and the reactor will cease operating. If, on the other hand, the burnable poison is depleted before the fuel is burned up, the chain reaction process will need additional means of control and the reactor operation will have to be interrupted. This is a fairly slow process which can be foreseen well in advance. There are therefore no safety problems involved.

A design objective of the utmost importance for the reactor designer is to devise a fuel and adjoining burnable poison system which will permit refueling periods of 9–10 years. How this is achieved in practice in submarine fuel is not officially known. Such knowledge, however, is of public interest since the fuel design largely determines the 'Source Terms': the nature and the relative fractions of fission product inventory that may be released to the environment during and after an accident. The Source Terms of the different types of civilian fuel are known and will be discussed later on.

The burnable poison's readiness to bind reactivity raises a long-term safety question. A fuel core on the seabed subject to corrosion in the sea water might experience different corrosion rates in the fuel and the burnable poison sections. If the core structure is conserved and the burnable poison should corrode faster than the fuel, a second criticality, i.e. a re-start of the nuclear chain reaction, cannot be ruled out. The process will be a very slow one.

Development work on burnable poison technology was carried out in connection with the German civilian nuclear container ship project NCS-80 (which never materialized). In NS Otto Hahn's first and second fuel charges, boron was mixed with the uranium oxide fuel and served as burnable poison. This was not considered an entirely satisfactory solution. Difficulties with the homogenization process of uranium oxide and boron were observed. Another concept was to introduce the burnable poison as a central stringer in the fuel pin, see fig. 20.

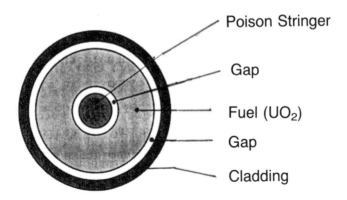

Fig. 20 Cross section through a fuel pin containing burnable poison.

Gadolineum-aluminate seems to be a better burnable poison than boron. It could be introduced into the fuel in very much the same way as that shown in fig. 20. The poison is mixed with aluminium oxide which acts as a matrix. This substance can be shaped into cylindrical pellets as in fig. 20 or it can be shaped into foils.

Civilian power plants use burnable poison too, but to a lesser extent than submarine fuel cores. Civilian power plant cores are therefore not particularly relevant for studies of submarine cores.

Is plutonium being used as submarine fuel?
Uranium-235 is the obvious submarine nuclear fuel. Nevertheless, plutonium-239 is an option. Can it be argued that plutonium is not being used? One main reason for **not** using plutonium is that weapon-grade plutonium has for a long time been in short supply in the nuclear weapons states. A distinct miniaturization of nuclear warheads during the two last decades has led to an increased use of plutonium instead of uranium. This has been particularly noticeable during the development of missiles with multiple warheads. Uranium warheads are heavier and more bulky. Increased attention to safety in handling nuclear weapons by introducing low-yield chemical explosives for triggering the bomb, also had as a consequence an increased use of plutonium.

The development of civilian fuel containing plutonium has progressed considerably over the last decade. Plutonium fuel is used on a commercial basis in French nuclear power plants, whereas other nations operate plutonium fuel on more of a pilot scale. This technique is probably not mature enough for submarines. In civilian uranium fuel with low enrichments, the uranium-oxide acts as the dispersing matrix material for the plutonium.

Nothing has been published on fuel designs with plutonium dispersed in any other type of matrix material. Such a design might well have been developed, but plutonium is a nasty element to work with. Uranium fuel is easier to develop and to handle. There is no compelling reason why a submarine nuclear power plant should also be a test bed for novel types of nuclear fuel. High reliability is a must in the operation of the nuclear plant. Nuclear submarines are therefore most probably fuelled by uranium and not by plutonium.

How does a propulsion plant operate?
A propulsion plant should ideally be able to operate in a natural convection circulation mode. The effect comes into play when warmer (and therefore lighter) water in the fuel channels is pressed out of the reactor core and up into the steam generator by the colder (and therefore heavier) water returning from the same generator. During natural convection circulation the weight difference between the two channels is the driving head. From a safety point of view, failures of the main pumps will have a minor effect on the operation of the plant if it can operate in a natural convection mode. Usually, strong pumps secure circulation. This driving head can be augmented by elevating the steam

generator relative to the reactor core. Within the cramped space of a submarine there is limited leeway for accommodating natural convection circulation. The tilting angle of the fuel relative to the vertical when the submarine sinks and rests on the seabed will reduce the driving head.

It is reported that the French Rubis class submarines can operate at normal cruising speeds in the natural convection circulation mode. If, however, the power plant should be operated at full capacity, the main circulation pumps are needed. The standard US propulsion plant S5W, designed as early as the 1960s, is able to operate in the natural mode. The British have been more sceptical about the blessings of the natural convection circulation mode. They were reportedly concerned that if slight boiling took place in the fuel channels, starting the pumps would have resulted in steam bubbles being swept out of the core. This could under certain circumstances lead to instabilities in the reactor operation. The French and US designs have apparently circumvented these problems.

There is another operating characteristic of a nuclear submarine worth considering. A military requirement is that the propulsion plant should respond rapidly to increased power demands. There are limitations to how fast a reactor's power level can be changed without damaging fuel elements through shock increases of heat generation. Such effects have been carefully studied for civilian nuclear power plants. As referred to above, the NS Otto Hahn plant had a permissible power level change of 4 percent per second, which is hardly acceptable for a submarine commander in an emergency combat situation. The limit will very much depend upon the fuel element design and is surely one of the primary specifications in the development of submarine fuel.

One way of circumventing this problem is to drain steam continuously directly to the condenser, bypassing the turbines. This drain could be as large as 15–20 percent of full power. To respond to an urgent demand, the drain could be switched directly to the turbine, giving the reactor time to catch up. The Soviets are apparently using this technique in their nuclear ice-breakers.

Noise: the Achilles heel of submarines

Emission of noise is the Achilles heel of any submarine. A nuclear propulsion plant aggravates this problem, where higher speeds and circulation pumps in the primary and secondary systems create noise. A substantial amount of work has been devoted to reducing noise emissions. Propulsion plant primary systems which are able to operate in the natural circulation mode are less noisy than systems with full use of circulation pumps. Lowering hydraulic resistance in the circuits adds to the reduction of noise.

Secondary circuits can be insulated from the hull by noise-suppressing mountings. Full scale mock-ups of pumping systems to be tested are also being used to study noise reduction techniques. Eliminating mechanical gears through turbo-electric drive systems promotes lower noise emission, while cladding the outside hull with anechoic tiles reduces reflections from active sonar. Proper design of the propellers can alleviate cavitation problems and noise emissions are accordingly reduced.

The noise emission levels of modern submarine designs have been substantially reduced compared to older designs. In particular some of the older Soviet submarines in the Hotel, Yankee, Echo and Alfa classes are noisy, whereas their new Victor III class is silent.

A nuclear 'race-horse': the liquid-metal cooled propulsion plant

Speed is armour. The Soviet nuclear submarine of the Alfa class has demonstrated speeds in excess of 40 knots and has hulls made of titanium. This was deduced from their lack of magnetic signature. A capacity for large diving depths was suspected. The relatively small displacement of the submarine, 3 700 tonnes, indicated that the Alfas were equipped with an entirely new type of propulsion source.

The need for propulsion plants with higher specific power
If the speed of a submerged submarine were increased from, say, 20 to 40 knots, the power increase necessary would not double, but increase by a factor of four. It is not possible to accommodate the corresponding weight and volume penalties resulting from such an expanded power plant within a normal submarine hull. Assuming that the weight reduction from using titanium instead of high-yield steel for the hulls was put back in the form of heavier hulls for greater diving depths, it seems that a propulsion source with a much higher specific power (megawatts per ton of propulsion plant weight) is being used.

The weight and volume of the primary system is not very sensitive to the reactor power level, irrespective of reactor type. The biological shielding will, within reason, be very much the same. The controlling factor, however, is the secondary power conversion system: the steam generators, steam turbines and main condenser. The specific power of the PWRs cannot be improved very much. Significant gains in specific power can be obtained only by increasing the temperature of the working fluid in the turbines and/or by lowering the exhaust pressure into the condenser (or both). Higher temperatures can hardly be obtained in PWRs, whereas lowering the condenser pressure will require a larger condenser surface in order to reject waste heat. Condensers are heavy and bulky.

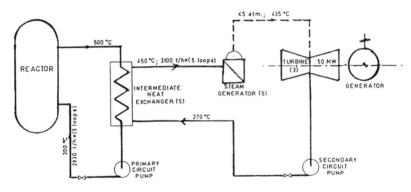

Fig. 21 Layout of the Soviet prototype 50 megawatt (electric) liquid-metal cooled propulsion plant BN-350.

One has to look for completely different solutions for the transport of heat energy out of a reactor with much higher specific power. Some liquid metals are very well suited for this purpose, since they can transport the thermal energy from the reactor fuel elements to the steam generators at higher temperatures than water can as used in the PWRs. From the steam generators, steam of high specific energy is transferred to the turbines.

The choice of liquid-metals for coolants
There are two liquid metals in use today: either sodium (Na), or a mixture of lead and bismuth. Liquid sodium is being used extensively in

fast-breeder nuclear power plants. The main disadvantage with sodium, however, is its violent chemical reaction with water. Liquid sodium cools the fuel elements and circulates through the primary side of the steam generators with water at their secondary side. The sodium technology is well advanced, and nuclear power stations based on it are in operation in France, the UK and in the Soviet Union.

Sodium has actually been used in nuclear submarines. The US Navy introduced a sodium-cooled propulsion plant in the early Sea Wolf class submarine. Construction of a prototype plant started in 1952 at West Milton near Schenectady, New York. The reactor was not strictly a fast breeder reactor. It is termed an 'intermediate' reactor in reference to the neutron velocity spectrum being intermediate between the usual pressurized water reactors and the true breeder reactors.

Sea Wolf was launched in 1955 and commissioned in 1957. She did not have a happy history. The superheaters in the plant were carefully designed to prevent sodium mixing with the water. Practical difficulties in assessing the adequacy of precautions taken led to the superheaters being bypassed altogether. A decision was ultimately made that the reactor plant should be replaced by an ordinary PWR plant. Since then no US propulsion plants have used liquid metals for cooling.

The propulsion plant in Sea Wolf was, however, not a total failure. Sea Wolf travelled a distance of 71 600 miles and in 1958 she remained submerged in the Atlantic for sixty days, longer than any other submarine to that day. The development of liquid-metal cooled propulsion plants was nevertheless abandoned in the US.

Sodium becomes extremely radioactive through absorption of neutrons in the reactor core. This radiation normally does no harm, being contained within the biological shielding. During maintenance there will be no problems either. The radioactive sodium isotopes decay rapidly.

The lead-bismuth alloy is also an excellent coolant. It is not as chemically reactive as the sodium coolant, though it is heavier. The reactor designer is faced with weight problems arising from the high density of the lead/ bismuth coolant. The reactor will probably be a breeder-type operating in a fast neutron fuel cycle. If so, the core can be made very compact with a high power density (kilowatts per liter). This reduces the demand for coolant. A reduction in the weight of the biological shielding should be possible due to the larger absorption of gamma-rays from the core in the heavy coolant.

The low complement (40) in the Alfa submarine indicates a highly automated control system with no need for operators working in the reactor area under operation.

The lead/bismuth eutecticum (0.55/0.45) melts at 45 °C. There must accordingly be a system for pre-heating the metallic coolant before start-up of the reactor. To the extent the solidified coolant surrounding the fuel is not corroded away it might serve as an additional barrier between the fuel and the environment.

The bismuth-209 isotope absorbs one neutron and is converted to bismuth-210, which is radioactive with a half-life of 5 days. Bismuth-210 decays to polonium-210. This is a most unpleasant substance, because of its alpha-activity with a half-life of 138.4 days. During normal operation, coolant spills, even when solidified, will create radiation dangers for the crew. This danger increases considerably during maintenance work on the primary system.

3 A survey of nuclear submarines

There is a large number of nuclear propelled ships in operation today
(1989), as shown in fig. 22 and in Table 1, see Appendix. About 400
submarines are deployed and 43 are under construction or on order.
They fall into various categories: ballistic missile submarines (SSBN),
guided missile submarines (SSGN) or attack or fleet submarines
(SSN). Other nuclear vessels are aircraft carriers and battle cruisers –
in total 17 vessels deployed and 7 under construction or on order. In
addition the Soviet Union has 6 nuclear ice-breakers and 1 nuclear
cargo ship in operation.

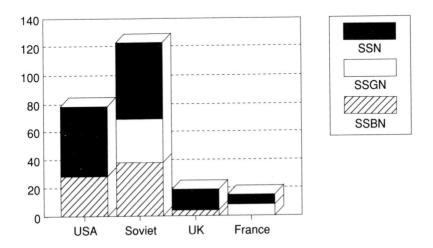

Fig. 22 Survey of nuclear submarines deployed in the North Atlantic 1989.

The vessels are distributed over the strategically important areas in the Atlantic and the Pacific as shown in Table 2.

	SSBN		SSGN		SSN	
	North Atl.	Pacific	North Atl.	Pacific	North Atl.	Pacific
United States	29	16	–	–	50	46
Soviet Union	38	25	30	19	55	25
United Kingdom	6	–	–	–	15	–
France	6	–	–	–	6	–

Table 2 Assumed distribution of deployed nuclear submarines between the Atlantic and the Pacific.

The loss rate of nuclear submarines in the Atlantic

The risks of nuclear accidents on the high seas are not proportional to the number of submarines deployed, but to the actual number of submarines in operation. US practice seems to be, (ref. 8), that standard patrol time for the SSBN's is 68 days with a subsequent 32 days of maintenance and training. Every six years major maintenance lasting two years is undertaken. Judging from these numbers, the availability of the SSBN submarines would be around 50 percent, meaning that at any one time half the submarine fleet is at sea. If the same applies to the other Western SSBN's, around 15 of them will continuously be at sea in the North Atlantic.

The availability of Soviet nuclear submarines is no doubt much lower than that of the other nuclear powers. In the 1960's they were hardly observed outside their domestic waters, though this situation has changed considerably in more recent years. The high rate of accidents indicates, however, that the Soviets do have problems with their submarines. An availability higher than 1/3, corresponding to 25 submarines, is therefore unlikely. In sum, more than 40 SSBN's and SSGN's are operating in the North Atlantic (including the Mediterranean) all year round.

For the US tactical nuclear submarines, the SSN's, similar reflections apply. The SSN's are subject to a major revision lasting 18 months every 7th to 9th year. Every second to third year, there are shorter maintenance periods. Crew training takes considerable time. It has been estimated that in theory the US SSN's are available 50 percent of the time, though this figure might be too high. Assuming an availability of 30 percent (ref. 8) and that this figure applies equally to the other navies, around 40 SSN's are available all the year round in the North Atlantic.

The potential risk of nuclear accidents in the North Atlantic should be evaluated from the continual, year-round presence of 80 nuclear submarines. A highly speculative loss rate for nuclear submarines on the high seas can be calculated, assuming an annual operation of 80 submarine-years per year over the 25 years since Thresher sank. This gives, with 2 000 operative submarine-years and a total loss of 6 submarines, an annual loss rate of 3 per 1 000.

Bearing in mind that Soviet nuclear submarines are equipped with two reactors, the total number of nuclear propulsion power plants deployed seems to be around 600. The power levels of the plants are, however, 30–40 times smaller than civilian nuclear power plants.

American nuclear submarine designs

Nuclear power for propulsion of submarines was at the outset not an obvious choice for the US Navy. The scepticism was subdued by the legendary Admiral Hyman G. Rickover, and a development programme for a nuclear propulsion plant started in 1949. A nuclear industry based on the Westinghouse, General Electric, Combustion Engineering and Babcock & Wilcox industries was established. The programme was a very broad one. Basic material problems had to be solved, particularly related to components exposed to intense radiation. Nuclear fuel able to sustain high burn-ups was a prerequisite in order to fully realize the potential benefits of nuclear propulsion.

The general approach

The Navy decided to construct full-scale prototypes of the various versions of propulsion plants in a shore-based test facility. The purpose of this was to thoroughly investigate the performance of the prototype in order to disclose weak points in design and operational characteristics. This procedure of testing and modifying designs before starting series production of the plants was essential to ensuring the safe operation of the submarines. All other nations adopted this design philosophy, except the Soviets. In the US programme several such prototype plants were constructed.

The various propulsion plants developed are labelled according to the formula AXB where A stands for the nuclear vessel type, X is the manufacturer's type number and B stands for the manufacturer – see the list below. S5W means therefore the fifth type of propulsion plant designed for submarines by Westinghouse.

A	B
S = Submarine	C = Combustion Engineering Inc
A = Carrier	G = General Electric Co
C = Cruiser	W = Westinghouse
D = Destroyer	

The initial development phase

The story of the nuclear propelled submarine starts with *Nautilus*. She was launched in 1954, equipped with an S2W propulsion plant with geared turbines. The power level was 70 megawatts, giving 7 500 shp to each of the two propellers.

Nautilus was not given the 'tear-drop' *Albacore* hull shape which at that time had been newly developed. One consideration had been not to complicate the design with many still unproven features. The first core lasted 2 700 hours at full power, the second 4 000 hours and the third was designed for 7 000 full-power hours. The first change of fuel took place after 2 years and the third charge after 4–5 years. Nautilus was driven 62 600 nautical miles (100 600 km) with the first charge, 91 300 nm (147 000 km) with the second and 150 000 nm (240 000 km) with the third.

Unlike the Soviets, the US Navy did not immediately embark on series production of submarines. Major development work was put into various improvements to the reactor system. Two reactor types, S3W and S4W, were tested in a limited number of submarines. S3W was tried in *Skate, Sargo* and *Halibut* (1957–60), while S4W propelled *Swordfish* and *Seadragon* (1958–59). The *Skipjack* class was based on the S5W plant with the same nominal thermal power, 70 megawatts, but with a higher thermal efficiency providing 15 000 shp to the propeller shaft. Skipjack was given an Albacore hull which enabled her to make exceptionally high speed submerged, 30 kts. This performance was considered to be outstanding. One submarine of the Skipjack class, *Scorpion,* was lost with all hands in the Atlantic in 1968 for unknown reasons.

The S5W propulsion plant was to become the 'work-horse' of the US

Navy until the 1970s. One important feature of this design was the extended use of redundancy of major components. There were two steam generators, two pressurizers, two sets of turbines and two sets of turbo-generators. Emergency homing power was secured by batteries and by diesel engines.

The attack submarines

In the early 1950s the US Navy pursued parallel development of attack submarines (SSN) for fleet work and submarines specifically designed for anti-submarine operations. *Tullibee* was constructed as an experimental submarine for the latter purpose. She was fitted with an S2C reactor delivered by Combustion Engineering Inc. This reactor was very small, 20 megawatts, giving 2 500 shp. A unique feature was the turbo-electric drive system which replaced the mechanical gear between the turbines and the propeller shaft.

The Tullibee line was not pursued further. The new attack submarine Thresher which succeeded the Skipjack class abandoned the turbo-electric drive system in favour of conventional geared turbines and the proven S5W reactor. The power level was apparently too small for this size of submarine. In an attempt to reduce noise, the reactor and gear were mounted on a 'raft' with resilient mountings. The pressure hull was the first to be built of HY80 high-yield steel, which permitted a maximum diving depth of 400 meters (1300ft). Thresher sank in 1962 during testing after the first refit. Improved construction technology seems to have eliminated problems in later ships of this class, now renamed the *Permit* class.

Sturgeon, equipped with an S5W propulsion plant, is the natural successor to the Permit class. Intensive development work was conducted on the improvment of reactor designs. A prototype sea-going natural convection circulation reactor, S5G, was installed in *Narwhal* which has a Sturgeon-type hull. S5G provides 70 megawatts or 17 000 shp to the propeller.

Los Angeles is an attack submarine. The first unit was completed in 1976 and at present 56 units are deployed with 10 more under construction. Displacement is 6 080 tonnes surfaced. She is equipped with an S6G propulsion plant providing 120 megawatts or 30 000 shp. This gives a maximum speed of 31 kts. The S6G plant is a modified version of the D2G reactor used to power missile destroyers since the early 1960s. It is able to sustain natural circulation of the coolant water, al-

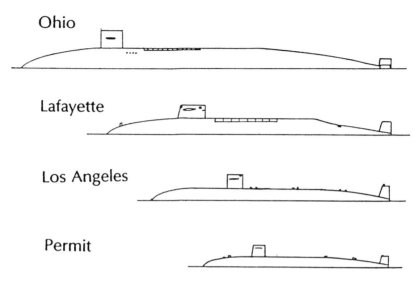

Fig. 23 Silhouettes of some American nuclear submarines. Ohio has a displacement of 18 750 tonnes submerged and a length of 560 feet (170.7 meters).

though circulation pumps have to be switched in at higher powers. Due to her large size, effective insulation of noise-generating equipment from the hull has been possible, making the Los Angeles very quiet.

A new class of attack submarines, the *Seawolf* class, is under construction. According to official statements this class will have: 'the highest tactical speed of any submarine we have ever built. It will have more weapons than any other attack submarine we have ever put to sea, and more than any Soviet attack submarine that has gone to sea. It will be the quietest submarine, because this will be the first submarine we have designed from the ground up in 20 years.'

The new Seawolf class will have a submerged displacement of 9 100 tonnes. She will be propelled by an advanced pressurised water reactor, the S6W, providing about 60 000 shp to the propeller. It is estimated that well over a billion dollars have been allocated for research and development. The Seawolf's speed will be close to that of the Soviet *Sierra* class, or 32–34 knots. The hull will most probably be built with HY130 steel. The Navy is said to be confident that the Seawolf class will be put to sea in 1994 in spite of contentions that the programme should be scrapped in favour of a different design.

The US Navy has pursued major development programmes in order to extend the submarine operating cycle, i.e. the period between major ship overhauls. The main motivation for doing so was twofold; firstly to improve ship operation availability, performance and flexibility, and secondly, to cut costs by reducing the number of shipyard overhauls. The cost of one overhaul is typically US$ 50 million.

The original operating cycle comprised alternating refuelling and non-refuelling overhauls, with an operating interval of 43 months and an overhaul duration of 12 to 18 months. Operating intervals have been extended from 43 to 84 months. The non-refuelling overhaul was eliminated, leaving a single refuelling outage during the entire ship's expected service life. Brief periods of restricted availability for maintenance are inserted between overhauls. Seawolf will have its operating interval extended beyond 15 years.

The ballistic missile submarines

The first ballistic missile submarines (SSBN) were converted Skipjacks. *Lafayette* became the standard US Navy SSBN until the *Ohio* class entered the scene. Lafayette carries Poseidon C3 missiles with a range of 2 500 nautical miles (nm). Twelve of the submarines have been converted to carry Trident C-4 missiles with a range of 4 000 nm. The change implies increased operational flexibility in the sense that these SSBNs are not then so dependent on forward deployment in European harbours. Lafayette is propelled by an S5W propulsion plant driving geared steam turbines.

The Ohio class submarines have a displacement (amount of sea water displaced by the ship's volume) of 18 750 tonnes submerged. They are the largest submarines built in the West. They carry ballistic Trident I C-4 missiles which will be replaced by Trident II C-5 now under development. The new SSBN class was originally intended to be an enlarged and improved Lafayette using S5W for propulsion. The US Navy, however, wanted a natural circulation reactor based on the plant tested in Narwhal and other noise-reducing systems. The increased expenditures were justified by increasing the number of missiles carried from 16 to 24.

The propulsion plant in Ohio, S8G, provides 220 megawatts or 60 000 shp to the propeller. The reactor drives two sets of turbines, one for high and the other for low speed. A turbo-electric drive system has been installed. All noise-emitting machinery is mounted on a raft and insulated from the hull. The reactor has a nuclear core life of about nine years between refuelings.

Soviet nuclear-propelled ships

The Soviet nuclear propulsion programme is a multi-faceted undertaking. Development work has followed different courses. One application to materialize very early was nuclear-propelled ice-breakers. Parallel independent development led to the first nuclear submarines. Another major effort has been the development of a liquid-metal-cooled reactor for ship propulsion. A further venture is the development of a nuclear-propelled cargo lighter carrier for operation in the Arctic.

The impact of shocks to major submarine plant components, simulating combat situations, are usually tested under laboratory conditions in large test facilities on shore. The Soviets have a unique technical opportunity in this respect since they have both submarine and ice-breaker propulsion plants simultaneously under development and in operation. Ice-breakers are important test beds for submarine plants.

General observations on how the Soviets embark on large projects are probably just as valid for their nuclear propulsion work. They are very pragmatic. The bureaucracy involved in changing or modifying a series production process is cumbersome. Even though it might conceivably be counterproductive to optimizing a new plant design, it is nevertheless easier to accept major components for a plant, i.e. steam turbines, steam generators etc., from an already existing series production, than to re-design the component from scratch, even if it is not fully adequate. One consequence could be deficiencies which could at least partly explain the poor performance of the Soviet Union's earlier propulsion plants.

Civilian nuclear-propelled ships

The Soviet Union has five nuclear propelled ice-breakers in operation and one under construction. *Lenin*, the first ice-breaker, was constructed during 1956–57 and started operation in 1959. The next one, *Arktika*, went into operation in 1974, and in 1977 the ice-breaker *Sibir* followed. *Rossiya* came in 1986. Arktika and Sibir are both equipped with two 135-megawatt PWR reactors providing 75 000 shp to the propeller.

Lenin was originally equipped with three reactors, one of which was considered a reserve. Each reactor had a power level of 90 megawatts. The power plant provided 44 000 shp to the propeller. Lenin is fairly well described in various references. The power plants left much to be desired. A major accident with loss of lives occurred in 1966 in one of the reactors which incapacitated the ship for several years. In 1970 the three reactors were replaced by two second-generation reactors of an improved design. Lenin is now withdrawn from active service.

The nuclear Arktika class ice-breakers have recently been severely criticised by the first captain of the Arktika, (ref. 9). In a letter to the Soviet shipping journal *Vodny Transport* he claims that the Arktika was 10 years out of date by the time she entered service in 1974. He says that the fifth and last of the Arktika class, the *Oktyabrskaya Revolutsiya*, not due to be completed until 1991, will by then be even more out of date.

In particular, the captain claims that the 75 000 shp output of the Arktika's steam turbines is only half of what is required to keep the northern sea route between the White Sea and the Pacific open longer than the present limited navigational season which runs from June to October. Plans for 150 000 shp nuclear ice-breakers have so far not materialized.

A nuclear propelled container-carrying ship, *Sevmorput*, has been constructed and is now operating. The ship is equipped with a 135-megawatt nuclear plant providing 40 000 shp to the propeller. The total displacement is about 61 000 tons. The primary plant is more or less fully standardized with the equipment of the nuclear powered ice-breakers. It has undergone practically no modifications compared to similar equipment in the Lenin and Arktika.

Nuclear submarines

The first generation of nuclear propulsion plants, constructed in the period 1956–62, were installed in the November, Echo and Hotel classes of submarines. The propulsion plant in the Hotel class was probably similar to the original plant in Lenin. Its power level, however, is lower, about 75 megawatts with 30 000 shp to the propeller, assuming an overall efficiency of 15 percent.

Contrary to the development in the United States, United Kingdom and France, no shore-based prototype apparently was constructed before the assembly-line production of the November class started. Whether this is an expression of negligence, underestimation or disrespect for the problems involved, or a desire to proceed at any cost, is a matter of speculation. Using whole classes of submarines as test beds in their development must have been immensely expensive, but the experiences gained must have provided more reliable statistics!

Neither was the *Victor* class, which appeared after an interval of four years, apparently preceded by a prototype plant. This could mean that the deviations from the first-generation plant were not that extensive. A consequence of this policy was that the performance of the first submarine classes was relatively poor. For many years they were hardly observed ouside their home bases. This improved later on.

Very little is known of the propulsion plants in the subsequent classes of submarines: *Yankee* I and II, *Delta* I, II, III and IV. They are equipped with plants yielding 50 000 shp. This could indicate a power level of 100 megawatts per reactor, assuming an overall efficiency of a little more than 20 percent. The *Charlie* class is the only Soviet submarine believed to have a single propulsion plant. If so, the power level should be around 170 megawatts. The Charlie class has been nicknamed 'The Chernobyl class' by the Indians due to their radiation-related problems. India has leased two Charlie I submarines from the Soviet Union.

A major step forward came with the construction of the *Typhoon* class submarines. They have a displacement of 25 000 tonnes and a speed of 30 knots submerged. There are seven of them in operation or under construction (the construction of the last one seems to have been stopped). This is the largest submarine ever built. It has two separate pressure hulls in parallel, which could be modified Delta hulls, covered by a single outer free-flood hull. There is a large stand-off between the outer and inner hulls along the sides, making them almost invulnerable to torpedo attacks. The pressure hulls are also well protected from damage in case of collisions and groundings.

The first submarine of this class was launched in 1980 and entered service in 1982. The propulsion plant is estimated to provide 80 000 shaft horse-power. *Jane's Fighting Ships* estimates that the two reactors each yield 330–360 megawatts of power. There are more likely to be 4 plants each yielding 170 megawatts. The *Oscar* class submarines with a

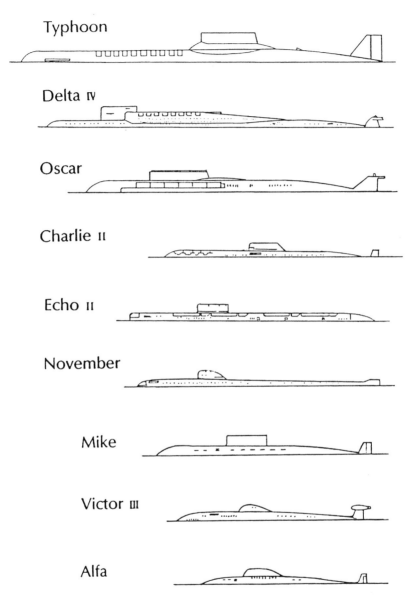

Fig. 24 Silhouettes of some Soviet nuclear submarines. The Typhoon is the largest submarine ever built with a displacement of 25–30 000 tonnes and a length of 558 feet (170 meters).

displacement of 16 000 tonnes dived, and 90 000 shp to the propellers, are apparently equipped with the same power plants.

The *Alfa* class of submarines represents a different tack in the development process. The Alfas are fairly small attack submarines with exceptionally high speeds, 45 knots dived. The propulsion plant is believed to be liquid-metal cooled. This gives a higher thermal efficiency and therefore lower demand for dissipation of waste heat. *Jane's* estimates that the Alfas have 47 000 shp to the propeller. Alfa is turbo-electrically propelled by a single shaft 35 megawatt electric motor. It is difficult to assess the thermal efficiency of the liquid-metal cooled propulsion plant, but, assuming it to be 30 percent, a power level of 60 megawatts per reactor seems reasonable.

Alfas are no longer being built. They are quite expensive. The Soviets have given them the pet name *golden fishes*, apparently because of high unit cost. They are quite noisy, and the design is, after all, 25 years old. The individual Alfas might all be different, indicating that they are part of a development programme from which the Sierra and Mike classes have benefitted. One interesting feature is the low manning level, about 40, indicating a high level of automation in the propulsion system.

Mike was launched in 1983 and entered service in 1984. She has a displacement of 6 400 tonnes dived and has possibly a titanium hull like the Alfas. Mike has been assumed to be a test vessel for new propulsion technology based upon a liquid-metal cooled propulsion plant. The tragedy in the North Atlantic in April 1989 when a Mike, the *Komsomolets*, sank after a fire with the loss of 44 men, has left some unanswered questions on this aspect. The official statement from the Soviet authorities in May 1989 made it clear that the propulsion plant was not a liquid-metal cooled reactor but a pressurized water reactor with modestly-enriched uranium fuel.

Some light is shed on this in an open letter on behalf of the survivors to the newspaper *Komsomolskaya Pravda* from three members of the crew. The three complain about the information given to the public concerning the accident and describe it as subjective, biased and without documentation. *Komsomolets* was not an old submarine. Nevertheless, a decision had been taken in 1988 to withdraw the vessel from active service. (This might explain why the Mike did not get any followers. The design must have been a failure.) The unique feature about *Komsomolets* was not the material used for its construction, but the ability to dive to a depth of 1 000 meters and stay there for sustained periods, it was said.

Nuclear military surface ships

The Soviet Union has two nuclear powered battle cruisers, the *Kirov* class, in operation and two under construction. The first was commissioned in 1980. Kirov has a displacement of 28 000 tonnes full load. Two PWR reactors and oil-fired boilers together provide 150 000 shp. The oil-fired boilers provide a superheating capability which may boost the steam output by about 50 percent. Kirov is designed for high speed, which can be deduced from the shape of the hull and the large propellers. Assuming that the Soviet PWR reactors are standardized and that Kirov has two 330–360 megawatt or 4x170 megawatt thermal units, these will contribute with about 90 000 horse-power to the propeller giving a speed of 24–25 knots. This is the same propulsion power as in the Typhoon and Oscar classes. The remaining 60 000 shp and hotel and equipment loads must then be derived from the oil-fired boilers, increasing the speed to 32 knots maximum. The nuclear part could, however, be larger.

Kirov experienced some difficulties with one of the reactors while cruising in the Mediterranean Sea in January 1990. A minor leakage in the primary system occurred. Kirov returned to the homebase at Kola on its own power.

Two nuclear propelled aircraft carriers have been launched, the first one in 1985 and the second in 1988. Sea trials of the first could take place in 1989. The displacement is 65 000 tonnes and they will probably be powered with 2 PWRs. Approximately 200 000 shp is anticipated.

British nuclear submarine programme

The British nuclear submarine programme has been focused on the indigenous development of the nuclear propulsion plant PWR-1 and its subsequent improved version PWR-2, (10).

The initial phase

The initial phase was the preparatory work with the establishment of supporting experimental facilities. It started in 1954 with an extensive research and development work for the *Valiant* class submarines. A landbased prototype submarine propulsion-plant was constructed as a major tool to develop the technology. The Dounreay Submarine Marine Plant (DS/MP) was located at the Royal Navy Vulcan test site adjacent to the Dounreay Research Centre in North Scotland. This plant was completed in 1963.

The operation of DS/MP was vital to the understanding of the engineering problems related to plant design. The main emphasis had been on the primary (reactor, nuclear fuel, steam transformer etc.) plant functions. The secondary plant with steam turbines, condensers etc. was considered to represent a reasonably well-proven technology with problems that could be solved in due course. This turned out to be a misconception, as in fact most of the problems turned up in this sector. The main source of trouble stemmed from the choice of construction materials and from the layout of pumps, condensors and sea-water cooling, being subject to the strict limitations imposed by hull dimensions.

Leaks developed as a result of poor welding of joints. All were related to weld areas in nickel-alloy pipework. Examination revealed that the weaknesses had occurred due to stress-assisted intergranular corrosion cracking. The presence of chlorine from sea water turned out to be a larger problem than anticipated. Extensive development work aimed at solving these problems was not successful, and a major refit of the secondary system was necessary.

Another major task of the DS/MP plant was to irradiate the prototype uranium fuel charge in order to assess its integrity for long-lasting irradiation.

In 1958 the United Kingdom entered into a collaboration agreement with the United States. This agreement entitled the UK to purchase one complete submarine nuclear propulsion plant, US S5W, with enriched uranium fuel and with a once-and-for-all technology transfer. This plant was installed in the HMS *Dreadnought* which went to sea in 1963.

The PWR-1 propulsion plant

Development of the 70-megawatt PWR-1 power plant was a pivot of the submarine programme. The programme included extensive development work on an evolutionary series of fuel element designs and the construction of an engineering plant to handle all installation problems related to series production of propulsion plants. Three generations of this PWR-1 propulsion plant are in operation today. An overview of the British nuclear submarine development programme is presented in (ref. 10), fig. 25.

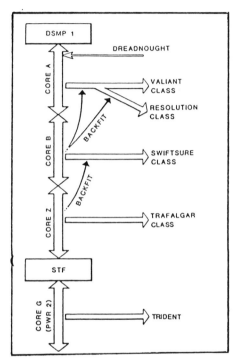

Fig. 25 British nuclear propulsion development 1955–89.

An important feature of the total programme is the flexibility introduced from the very beginning to permit the refitting of major components like reactor fuel.

The *Valiant* class submarines
The first British-designed nuclear submarine HMS Valiant benefitted from the experience gained from both the shore prototype plant DS/MP and the American S5W plant. The Valiant propulsion plant PWR-1 differed in many respects from the DS/MP. All nickel-alloy piping and fittings in chromium-molybdenum low-alloy steel were replaced with stainless steel. Primary circuit and main plant components were

fabricated in stainless steel using US design codes for pressure pipings and components. The reactor pressure vessel consisted of a low-alloy steel lined with stainless steel deposited by weld deposition.

The *Resolution* class

At the Nassau Conference in 1962, the United States undertook to provide missiles and associated systems for a British submarine deterrent force. The warheads and the submarines themselves were to be of British design. In February 1963 orders were placed for four *Polaris* submarines with nuclear propulsion plants based on the Valiant design. HMS Resolution was the first in this class. She has a displacement of 8 500 tonnes submerged and is equipped with a PWR-1 propulsion plant which provides 15 000 shp.

All the trouble-shooting from the Valiant/DSMP design has ensured that the Resolution class inherited a tested and proven propulsion plant, albeit one – it has been claimed – that initially required a high degree of maintenance to keep it fully operational.

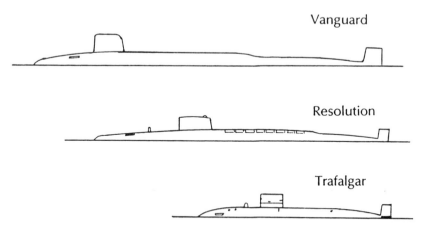

Fig. 26 Silhouettes of some British nuclear submarines. Vanguard has a length of 486.4 feet (148.3 meters).

The *Swiftsure* class submarine

A second-generation PWR-1 type propulsion plant design was introduced into the Swiftsure class. The second-generation plant was not to be a revolutionary new design, but an evolutionary advance from the Valiant design with emphasis on improved machinery arrangement, ease of operation and maintainability. The installation, operation, maintenance and overhaul procedures of the Valiant propulsion plant, particularly of the secondary machinery, were very complex. Some systems, such as the intricate and widespread auxiliary sea-water cooling system fitted in Valiant, not only presented the operators with a heavy maintenance load in terms of cooler fouling and problems with the mechanical seals on the pumps, but a failure of such a system at depth put the submarine at risk; it has been reported (ref. 10) that this kind of failure could lead to the loss of the submarine.

The primary system plant of Valiant, however, had an excellent record. The apparent reason was that it was recognized from the very beginning that high reliability was a pre-requisite for nuclear safety. Achieving high reliability through production quality control and quality assurance was one of the important lessons learnt in the US submarine programme and adapted by the British.

In 1967 a new fuel-charge design, designated core B, was installed in the test reactor DS/MP for two years' irradiation. The purpose of this was to achieve significant fuel burn-up and to ensure confidence in the design prior to committing the Swiftsure core for production. The experience from the Valiant development was that the operation of DS/MP had two functions which conflicted with each other. Continuous full power for fuel irradiation was not in harmony with the need for an on-off operation to test the secondary system. Prototype testing of the secondary system plant was therefore carried out in the Admiralty Development Establishment Barrow close to the shipyard. Colliding interests between the respective needs for performing substantive long-term prototype plant testing, and production testing of follow-on submarine machinery sets, led to the founding of the Submarine Machinery Installation Test Establishment (SMITS).

The Swiftsure was launched in January 1971 and accepted into service by the Royal Navy in 1973. She has a displacement of 4 900 tonnes dived. Operating experience from the Swiftsure class confirmed the design changes from the Valiant class propulsion plant. The plant's reliability, reflecting the simpler machinery arrangement enhanced by the higher quality of design, fabrication and installation work, turned out to be much better than the original design targets.

One of the submarines of this class, *Sceptre*, finished a complete overhaul in 1987. She was then fitted with a *Z* core giving a 12-year life cycle, although refit/refuel cycles will remain at 8–9 year intervals.

The *Trafalgar* class submarines
The Trafalgar is powered by a third-generation PWR-1 nuclear plant which, with two General Electric geared steam turbines, yields 15 000 shp. An important design objective for the reactor plant was to increase through-life utilization of the submarine by reducing the number of major refueling refits. Development work on the Trafalgar class primary plant therefore was aimed at achieving an increased core life. A fuel charge labelled *core Z*, see fig. 25, was installed in the test reactor DS/MP, following a major refit of the complete propulsion plant at Dounreay in 1973/74.

As described earlier, temperature variations due to frequent power changes are a key feature of nuclear propulsion plants. The need to achieve extended core life brought into prominence thermal fatigue in certain pipework and fittings. Extensive research resulted in improved methods of detail design in order to eliminate susceptibility to thermal fatigue. It was discovered that under certain loading conditions incipient cracking could occur from thermal variations of as little as 10 °C.

The Trafalgar is designed to be considerably more silent than previous submarines. Great attention was directed towards reductions in the radiated and self-noise spectra of the propulsion plant. This was obtained by reductions in the pumping power and the noise at source of the main coolant pumps. The pressure hull and outer surfaces are coated with wrap-around sound absorbing tiles.

The PWR-2 propulsion plant
A thorough assessment of the relative merits of the dispersed versus the integrated reactor design started in 1972. Advantages were counterbalanced by disadvantages. The original ambitions for an integrated reactor concept included saving space and weight as well as noise reduction. They were not fully realizable. In 1976, therefore, design effort was transferred to the development of a new design for a dispersed PWR plant. The Admiralty Board objectives were, firstly, to enhance safety margins; secondly, to improve the plant design for in-service inspection; and thirdly, to improve military characteristics in the form of increased power, lower noise, improved shock resistance and increased core life.

The reactor design which evolved became known as the PWR-2. It has a power level about twice that of the PWR-1, or 130 megawatts. Substantial changes were made in all major components and their arrangements. The PWR-2 features provide for less noise from coolant pumps, greater shock resistance under attack and a reduced need for maintenance. Full prototype testing was required. The development programme called for building a second Shore Test Facility (STF2) on the same site as the existing DS/MP. This facility was built in time to ensure sufficient testing and fuel burn-up prior to ordering the first production core for a new class of submarines.

The original shore test facility, DS/MP, has been converted to a loss-of-coolant experimental test facility, LAIRD. The experiments will probably also be of interest for the civilian nuclear power stations which have power levels 25–30 times larger. LAIRD will be used to simulate the safety systems of current and future reactor technology for the Navy. Dummy fuel, electrically heated, simulates the real thing. In such a facility, the effects of loss of coolant can be studied for specific nuclear fuel configurations.

The *Vanguard* class submarines

In 1980 the British Government announced its intentions to procure from the US the *Trident* 1 nuclear weapon system comprising the C4 ballistic missile and supporting system for a force of new British missile-launching submarines. They will replace the Polaris submarines in the 1990s. In 1982 the Government opted to procure the Trident II system with the D5 missile to be deployed in four submarines in the mid 1990s. The first submarine Vanguard was ordered in 1986. The Vanguard class has a displacement of 15 000 tonnes dived and is powered by a PWR-2 yielding 27 500 shaft horse-power. The refit and re-core interval is anticipated to be 8–9 years.

The *SSN20* class submarines

The next generation of the Royal Navy's nuclear-powered fleet of submarines is now on its way. In 1987 Vickers Shipbuilding Ltd was awarded a contract to carry out design work for the SSN20 or *W* class submarine.

The SSN20 class is considered to be similar to the US Seawolf class. The submarine will be powered by the PWR-2 reactor plant which is expected to have an output in excess of 22 500 shp. An order for the first of this class is planned for 1990, for laying down in 1992 and commissioning in 1997. The displacement is about 5 000 tonnes.

The French nuclear naval programme

French nuclear submarine development was started in 1959. Le Groupe de Propulsion Nucléaire (G.P.N) was established within the framework of the Commissariat à l'Energie Atomique (CEA). The first mission of the G.P.N. was to design and construct a landbased prototype, le Prototype à Terre (P.A.T.), for a nuclear submarine propulsion plant. The prototype went into operation in 1964 at le Centre d'Etudes Nucléaire, Cadarache, in southern France.

The first of a series of six strategic nuclear submarines, *le Redoutable* went to sea in June 1969 followed by five others in the period up to 1984. A seventh S.N.L.E-N.G (New Generation), *le Triomphant*, will benefit from the work done on improving nuclear power plant designs for a new generation of propulsion plant, type K15 yielding 150 megawatt. The nuclear propelled aircraft carrier, *Charles de Gaulle*, presently under construction (Porte-avions Nucléaire P.A.N.) will be fitted with two of these plants giving 82 000 shp on two shafts. The speed will be 27 knots which is rather slow for an aircraft carrier. A primary consideration was to reduce costs by avoiding the development of a new reactor design.

In August 1974 the nuclear propulsion work was taken over by *Technicatome*, which is a subsidiary organisation of CEA. One objective was to advance civilian applications of the technology developed for propulsion purposes, i.e. low-power nuclear plants for electricity and heat supplies. A special nuclear reactor plant, la Chaufferie Avancé Prototype (C.A.P.), started operating in Cadarache in November 1975. This is an efficient reactor plant of an integrated design utilized for the further development of a second-generation propulsion plant. This second-generation plant is now utilized in the series of seven nuclear attack submarines starting with le Rubis, which was commissioned in February 1983. Three others have followed.

The layout of the propulsion plant of Rubis is shown in fig. 27. The plant must be very compact since it is accomodated within a pressure hull of diameter 7.6 meters. The primary integrated circuit is shown in A, the secondary electric power generating plant in B and the electric

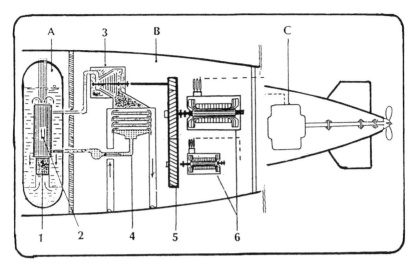

Fig. 27 Layout of the power plant of the French nuclear attack submarine Rubis. The Rubis is the smallest nuclear submarine ever built. Her displacement is 2 500 tonnes. She was commissioned in 1983. The length of the vessel is 72 meters and the diameter is 7.6 meters. The propulsion plant yields 48 megawatt thermal.

populsion motor in C. The reactor core (1) and steam generator (2) are situated within the pressure vessel. Primary pumps are not shown in the figure, but the arrangement permits reactor operation under natural convection circulation conditions. Steam turbines with condensor are shown in (3) and (4), and the mechanical gear in (5). There are two turbo-alternators, one supplying power for the propulsion motor and a second provides power for all auxiliary equipment, including the reactor plant which consumes a considerable amount of power for the pumps.

Proliferation of nuclear submarines

A sidetrack to the main theme of this book, but nevertheless an important one, is the 'proliferation' now observed of nuclear submarines in other countries. On the grounds that prevention is better than cure, this proliferation should be stopped.

In 1988 India leased a nuclear-powered cruise missile submarine of the Charlie I class from the Soviet Union and a second submarine of the same class early in 1990. It is rumoured that this is a replacement for the first one which are reported to have radiation related problems. India has now decided to cancel plans to acquire six Charlie I class submarines. India is likely to return the two submarines already received.

India has its own development programme on nuclear propulsion. Indian policy for years has been to preserve political independence, being self-supported in supplies and to rely on indigenously developed industrial technology. Having marine vessels with nuclear propulsion could therefore be looked upon not only as a token of the nation's resolve to increase its presence in the Indian Ocean, but also of its intention to exploit for propulsion purposes the extensive expertise in nuclear technology which has been developed within the civilian nuclear power programme.

Argentina has aspired for a number of years to develop nuclear submarines. The Argentinian Navy's interest both in nuclear weapons and in nuclear propulsion has been manifest through heavy recruitment to top management posts in the Argentinian Nuclear Energy Commission.

Brazil has ambitions for a strong presence in the South Atlantic. This ambition leads Brazil, according to a spokesman for the Brazilian Navy, *in a firm, prudent and deliberate fashion, to the nuclear powered submarine*, (ref. 12). The experience gained from the Falklands War has increased Argentinian as well as Brazilian interests in nuclear propulsion. The Brazilian military command was apparently impressed by the efficiency of the British nuclear submarines. After the tragic sinking of the Argentinian cruiser *General Belgrano*, the Argentinian Navy pulled out of the combat zone. The vulnerability of the British expeditionary force if a corresponding Argentinean counter-threat had been possible, must have been a tempting dream for the Argentinian military command.

The development of a Brazilian nuclear submarine is part of a research programme being conducted by the Institute of Energy and Nuclear Research at the University of São Paulo. The Brazilian Government has earmarked land in the town of Ipero, near Sarocaba, State of São Paulo, for the Navy for the construction of a naval nuclear research facility.

The Brazilian submarine study project is concentrated on a nuclear vessel of 2700–3000 tonnes with a speed in the range of 25–30 knots. The Chairman of the Brazilian Nuclear Research Commission has stated that uranium enrichment technology is the principal aspect of their nuclear submarine development project. In September 1987, Brazil announced that it had mastered the enrichment process.

Canada had in 1989 planned to strengthen its naval forces by buying 10–12 nuclear submarines (ref. 13). There were two options, either to buy the British Trafalgar class or the French Amethyste class. The cost of the programme was estimated to be $8 billion. The nuclear plant technology in the Trafalgar is essentially British. The French offered to co-develop with Canada a successor to the Amethyste class as part of their bid.

The new Canadian Government with its Prime Minister B. Mulroney decided in April 1989 to drop the whole project due to the high cost of the programme and because it was not felt to be necessary. The Canadian Navy will instead be strengthened by other major investments.

☆☆☆

Any sovereign nation has the right to defend its national integrity and security by whatever military means as are deemed appropriate (within the limits of certain humanitarian conventions), including nuclear weapons. A number of nations have abstained from the right to develop, acquire or possess nuclear weapons by signing the Non-Proliferation Treaty for Nuclear Weapons (NPT). Will the use of nuclear energy for propulsion of marine vessels be a violation of the NPT? Definitely not, neither in letter nor in spirit.

There is, however, a real danger that the proliferation of nuclear submarines will spur the arms race in regions where they are introduced. They will be regarded as 'just ordinary weapons'. There will be no 'barriers' against their use in regional conflicts, as is the case with nuclear weapons. In fact, the British *Conqueror* was the first nuclear submarine to fire a shot in anger when she sank the Argentinian cruiser *General Belgrano* in May 1982. A deliberately sunk and damaged nuclear submarine in a regional conflict could cause a local environmental pollution disaster, depending on where and how it happened.

The Canadian decision to abstain from buying or co-developing nuclear submarines is, in this context, an encouraging one. The proliferation problem of nuclear submarines ought to be on the agenda of the United Nations Committee for Disarmament.

Part two

– the risks –

A number of factors influence the risks and safety of nuclear submarines. The risks arise from the amounts of radioactive material present in the nuclear propulsion plant and nuclear weapons and safety barriers have been introduced to ensure maximum control in all emergency situations. Nevertheless, accidents do occur, and potential accident scenarios, which to some extent have actually happened – and which might happen again tomorrow – illustrate the magnitude and nature of the risks.

4 Factors influencing the accident risks and the safety of nuclear submarines

The assessment of risks with nuclear submarines has to include evaluations of operational safety margins.

To which depths can submarines dive?

Operating depths are usually referred to as:

a) normal operating depth
b) maximum operating depth
c) maximum calculation depth (collapsing depth)

The interrelationship between these parameters is described in Heggstad (ref. 14). There are bound to be uncertainties related to any mechanical engineering structure. To be on the safe side, the intended maximum load has to be multiplied by an estimated safety factor to stipulate a 'calculation load'. This safety factor could be given a value between 1 and 10. For submarine pressure hulls it is generally between 1.5 and 2.5. This factor usually includes a certain margin to allow for a recovery manoeuver in the event of the submarine accidentally diving beyond its maximum allowed operation depth.

According to Heggstad (ref. 14) the maximum operating depth multiplied by the safety factor should be called 'calculation depth' or 'calculation pressure', not 'collapse depth' as is frequently the case. Calculation depth might, however, be within 10 percent of the collapse depth.

The safety factor has a 'dynamic' as well as a 'static' component depending on the manoeuverability and also on the length of the submarine. This is illustrated in fig. 28 (ref. 14). The strength of the hull against underwater explosions at a given depth is called the residual pressure strength.

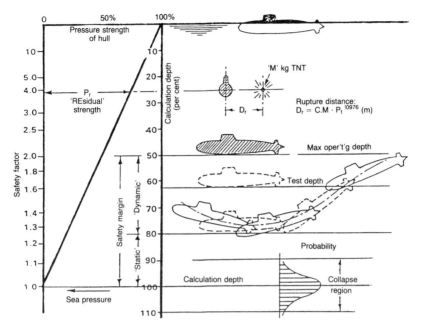

Fig. 28 The relationship between different terms used for depth and safety.

Information on maximum depth values is bound to be secret, so the interpretation of published values is therefore uncertain. Some values found in various references are given in Table 3.

Submarine class	Norm.op depth (meter)	Max.op. depth (meter)	Max. calc. depth (meter)
Ohio (US)	300		
Los Angeles (US)	450		
Sturgeon (US)	400		
Trafalgar (UK)	>175		
Rubis (FR)	300		
November (S)	400	500(?)	
Echo-II (S)	400	450(?)	
Victor I,II and III	400		
Alfa (S)	600	900(?)	1350?
Charlie I/II	400	600	
Mike		1 000	

Table 3 Operating depths of some submarines.

The high operating-depth figures quoted for the Alfa and Mike classes are attributed to the titanium-alloy construction material of the hull.

Safety precautions taken by design measures

A nuclear submarine's vulnerability to accidents or collisions depends on the degree and sophistication of the safety precautions built into the submarine design. The International Maritime Organization (IMO) Code of Safety certainly does not cover military objectives of submarines, but it reflects sound engineering principles which should at least represent minimum requirements for submarine design. The following engineered safety precautions will be described below:

– Safety barriers 1–4
– Emergency core-cooling systems
– Shock-resistance measures
– One or two propulsion plants
– Double-hull structures

Safety barriers 1–4

The design of safety barriers is the most important engineered safety precaution. The barriers isolate the content of fission products in the reactor cores from the environment. They are described in the IMO Code for civilian maritime nuclear vessels, and could be considered equally relevant for submarines. In the words of the IMO Code (ref. 15):

Releases of radioactive products, under any Plant Process Condition (PPC), should be prevented or controlled to the dose-equivalent limits by the provision of a series of successive physical barriers between the nuclear fuel and the environment. This defence-in-depth concept requires that:
– the fuel cladding, which is the first barrier, has among its functions the safety function of retaining radioactive fission products from the fuel
– the primary pressure boundary, which is the second barrier, has among its functions the safety function of preventing the unintentional release of radioactive material from the primary system

– the containment structure, which is the third barrier and totally contains the primary pressure boundary, has as its principal role the safety function of limiting the leakage of radioactive material from any contained equipment, under any PPC, and

– the safety enclosure, which is the fourth barrier, surrounds the containment structure and any significant source of radioactivity associated with the NPP (Nuclear Propulsion Plant) and has as its principal role the safety function of preventing the unintentional release and limiting the leakage of radioactive material

In the following, engineering solutions fulfilling these criteria will be surveyed and an evaluation offered of the degree of possible breakdown of these barriers during accidents and collisions. Of course, the actual state of these barriers is very sensitive military information. One has to resort to generic information, which is helpful to some extent. Some information can be inferred from civilian nuclear power stations, from Soviet ice-breaker designs and from civilian nuclear-propelled cargo-ships including the Soviet container carrier.

The four barriers are shown in principle in fig. 29.

The first barrier

The first barrier consists of the fuel 'meat' and cladding which has been described in chapter 2. It should be stressed that each fuel pin (or plate) is individually clad. In a reactor core there may be more than 10 000 pins. If the cladding should crack in a single pin, the content of this pin only can be released to the reactor primary system.

The fuel 'meat' proper has in addition an ability to retain fission products. The extent of release will depend on the volatility of the individual fission products and the temperature of the fuel.

The second barrier

The second barrier consists of the walls which contain the primary coolant water under pressure, i.e. the walls of the pressure vessel, the primary pumps, the pressurizer, the steam generator and the pipes connecting them. The crucial issue is the integrity of the system with respect to severe shocks. It is believed that the pressure vessel itself will withstand any conceivable shock, whereas the tubes connecting the pressure vessel with steam generators, pressurizers and main circulation pumps are vulnerable. A break in this tubing might lead to a

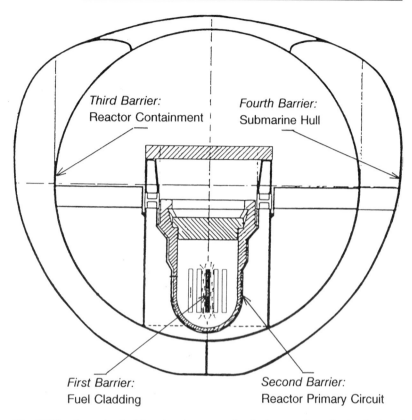

Third Barrier:
Reactor Containment

Fourth Barrier:
Submarine Hull

First Barrier:
Fuel Cladding

Second Barrier:
Reactor Primary Circuit

Fig. 29 The four physical barriers between the fission products in the fuel and the environment: the fuel cladding, the reactor primary system boundary, the containment structure and the safety enclosure.

Loss Of Coolant Accident (LOCA). No information is available on how the primary system in submarine plants has been designed to resist and absorb external shocks. The choice between a loop and an integrated plant design has certainly been influenced by the system's ability to resist external shocks.

The third barrier
The third barrier, the containment structure, is a tank which contains the entire primary system. There are basically two ways of dimensioning a containment structure: either to design it to take the 'full pressure load' if there is a full-scale blow-down of the coolant in the reactor pri-

mary system, or to provide for a 'pressure suppression system', see fig. 30. Containment structures are described in the safety reports of NS Otto Hahn and NS Savannah. The containment structure in NS Otto Hahn is of the first category, which can support the full pressure increase if the primary system breaks down. The containment structure of the Soviet lighter carrier has a pressure suppression system. The design of submarine containments is not known, but they are most likely equipped with pressure suppression systems.

The containment structure of the Soviet cargo ship (ref. 16) consists of flat sections of high-tensile sheet steel, 35 mm thick, with vertical supporting ribs. The structure is divided into a reactor room and an equipment room. All the primary system equipment is located in the reactor room under biological shielding made in the form of removable concrete blocks, see fig. 30.

Personnel enter the reactor and equipment rooms through airlocks fitted with pressurized doors with interlocks preventing them being opened simultaneously. For repair work and recharging of the fuel core, the containment structure has a hatch cover which allows for vertical transportation of the primary system equipment being replaced. The hatch cover is sealed with a welded joint.

Filters are installed in the bypass of the system's exhaust circuit, which close upon detection of air contamination within the containment. Automatic quick-closing valves are installed in the system's exhaust and intake ducts. These will cut off the containment in an emergency if pressure reaches 8 kilopascals. These measures for sealing off the containment structure preclude the uncontrolled discharge of radioactive substances into the space adjacent to the containment structure or to the environment under any emergency situations involving a major loss of coolant.

The fourth barrier
The fourth protective barrier – the safety enclosure – is intended to prevent the release of radioactive substances from all sources to other parts of the vessel. The limits of the safety enclosure are the longitudinal and transverse bulkheads of the reactor compartment and the hull. In accordance with the IMO Code the safety enclosure must completely surround the containment structure and all real sources of radioactivity. The reactor unit's auxiliary-circuit equipment, important equipment for the safety and electrical power distribution systems, as

well as equipment for systems for the collection, storage and removal of liquid and solid radioactive waste are located in the safety enclosure. All rooms in the safety enclosure are divided into conditional zones in concordance with the Code in order to prevent the spread of radioactive substances beyond their limits. There are three types of zones: 'monitored', 'observed' and 'free'. Passage into the monitored and observed zones is through a compulsory medical check point entailing a complete change of clothing and personal cleansing.

The pressure and external hulls of the submarine are substantial parts of the safety enclosure. The external hull protects the pressure hull. The stand-off between the two hulls can be very wide for the later Soviet submarines of the Oscar and Typhoon classes. There is a large number of penetrations in the pressure hull for all kinds of purposes such as personnel hatches, torpedo tubes, propeller shafts, cooling water supplies and for instrument cables. The penetrations, amounting to 100 or more, are of course carefully sealed, but might be expected to deteriorate faster than the hull itself if it should come to rest forever on the seabed. For that reason the penetrations are potential leakage sites.

The emergency core-cooling system

The second set of engineered safety precautions is the emergency core-cooling system. Such systems exist in all civilian power plants, and they have to be a part of submarine reactors as well. Again one has to resort to the description of civilian propulsion plants.

In the Soviet cargo-ship propulsion plant there is one system for 'pressure suppression' in a full blow-down (loss of coolant accident) in the containment structure, and another system for 'fuel emergency flooding'. Their purpose is to reduce the consequences of the most extreme accidents, fig. 4.3.

The first system provides for passage of the steam and air formed in an accident from the containment spaces into a cofferdam through a bubbling tank, which condenses the steam. The pressure of the steam/air mixture within the containment then drops due to steam expansion and condensation. The safety plugs react at a pressure increase of 0.15 megapascals in the reactor and equipment room, and the steam/air mixture is then led through the overflow ducts into the bubbling tanks. The pressure limit under extreme circumstances in the containment is set at 0.18 megapascals.

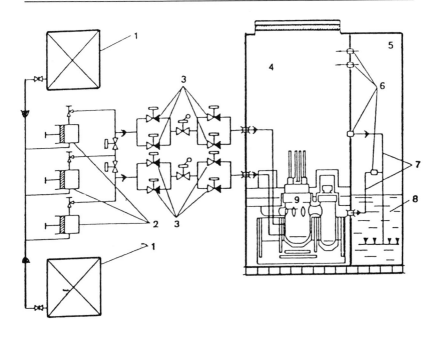

1. Feed Water reserve tank
2. Flooding pump
3. Emergency flooding valve
4. Equipment room
5. Cofferdam
6. Safety plugs
7. Overflow ducts
8. Bubbling tank
9. Reactor room

Fig. 30 Containment structure with pressure-suppression and flooding systems in the Soviet nuclear-propelled civilian cargo ship.

Depending on available emergency power, the second system, the fuel flooding system, will supply water to the primary system with a delivery rate which precludes exposure of the fuel core. The system consists of three flooding pumps with a capacity of 20 m³/hr each and a delivery pressure of 10 megapascals. On the signal indicating a drop of pressure in the primary system, two flooding pumps are activated. The pumps take water from the two feed-water reserve tanks and supply the primary system through two autonomous mains via two full-pass valves installed in parallel on each main. If one of the pumps fails to start, the third reserve pump starts automatically and is connected to the main of the unit which did not start. The fuel emergency flooding system prevents the fuel cladding being destroyed and thus substantially restricts the escape of radioactive fission products from the fuel to the coolant and then into the containment.

If the vessel sinks, the containment is flooded by means of ten flooding valves with pneumatic drives operating from an independent actuating air system. The valves are opened automatically when outside water pressure reaches 0.05 megapascals in the vicinity of the intake ducts on the upper deck. After the vessel settles on the seabed and pressure is equalized inside and outside, the containment and cofferdam are sealed again, preventing a mass exchange between the containment and external water masses.

The filling of the containment also permits the removal of afterheat from the fuel core when the vessel is flooded under conditions of a total absence of sources of electric power. In this case the fuel core is cooled by natural circulation of the primary system coolant. Heat is transferred from the coolant to sea water filling the reactor space of the containment, and natural circulation within the latter transfers heat through the containment walls to the surrounding medium. Both US and Soviet submarine plants are most likely fitted with 'pressure suppression' systems.

Shock-resistance measures

The third set of engineered safety precautions are design measures to increase shock resistance. It is presumed that detailed submarine design criteria exist in order to assure sufficient mechanical strength of components and systems against shocks. These criteria are, for obvious reasons, not known, but can be expected to be very strict.

Acceleration due to rapid bending caused by shocks might break equipment such as pipe valves, machinery and electronic equipment unless they are flexibly mounted. Shock protection therefore involves measures to reduce peak accelerations of equipment. Movement of pieces of equipment on their flexible mounts should not be so great that they hit each other or other solid structures.

The NS Otto Hahn safety report (17) quotes a shock-resistance capability of 1 g in all directions (g = gravitational acceleration). In order to make allowances for the maximum acceleration stresses (collision, groundings, etc.) in the region of the reactor, values of 1 and 2 g, respectively, were included in the calculations for the NS Savannah reactor plant and the cradle of the containment. These values are said to comply with the international estimates concerning maximum impact stresses (refs. 18 and 19).

One or two propulsion plants

The use of two propulsion plants can be considered a fourth set of engineered safety precautions. The question of reserve propulsion-power capacity is of paramount importance in all submarines. A two-reactor system is not necessarily the obvious or only solution. Developments have taken different courses in the Soviet and Western navies. In fact, the Soviet Union is the only nation predominantly with two propulsion plants in their submarines.

The Western nations rely on single plants. (In their surface ships there are two or more reactors). This reflects high confidence in the reliability of operation. The risk is, however, not negligible. The time required to restart a reactor is considerable.

Location of these reactors, separately or in a single machine room, is another design criterion. The freedom of choice in submarines is limited, indeed. Separate locations are hardly feasible, except in the largest submarines, but divided containment structures might be a possibility. In the larger vessels like Kirov, the Soviets nevertheless locate the reactors close to each other, as inferred from the photos of the ship. The Americans have their two or multiple reactor systems separated by a considerable distance.

Double hull structures

The use of double hulls is a fifth set of engineered safety measures. The Soviets make extensive use of double hulls. The added protection is of value only in the case of external events like collisions, in combat situations or groundings. Two hulls provide no added safety in the case of internal accidents.

Amounts of radioactive substances in a nuclear submarine

The reactor core inventory of radioactive fission products at any time is determined by constants of nature like the number of fissions per megawatt of power, how the uranium-235 nucleus splits up by fission (fission yields), the half-lives of the individual fission products (decay constants) and by the reactor operating power history. Details of a reactor's nuclear design are not so important, except that the fuel enrichment determines the build-up of plutonium isotopes.

Explanatory frame: The fission products

The nucleus of a uranium-235 atom is bound together by very strong nuclear forces. A consequence of this is that a great deal of energy is stored in the nucleus, which can be released if the nucleus is split (fissioned). If the nucleus is hit by a slowly moving neutron, it becomes unstable. Then two things might happen; either the nucleus calms down and converts to the isotope uranium-236, or the instability is so large that the nucleus is fissioned into two parts, each being an isotope of some other element. In addition, 2 or 3 neutrons are emitted. The two parts are labelled 'fission products'.

Fission can occur in a large number of different ways, resulting in hundreds of different fission products. They are mostly unstable, with some of them emitting in rapid succession beta and gamma radiation until they reach a stable or semi-stable configuration with distinct 'half-lives'.

The fission products and the neutrons are very energetic and carry away the surplus energy in the uranium-235 nucleus. The fission products collide with other uranium atoms and lose their energy rapidly. This energy appears as thermal heat and is the origin of the 'nuclear energy'.

When the fission products have come to rest in a reactor fuel element and have given their contribution to the nuclear energy function, they continue to release energy through their emission of beta and gamma rays. As long as the reactor is operating, this is a modest extra contribution to the reactor power level. When the reactor closes down, however, the fission products are the main heat source. This is the origin of the troublesome 'nuclear after-heat'.

Fission product inventory

The NS Savannah safety assessment (ref. 19) included 180 different fission products. Of them, 100 have half-lives of less than 1 hour. In addition, 34 fission products have half-lives between 1 hour and 1 day. About 40 fission products have longer half-lives; months to years. The total activity level at shut-down of the reactor is halved in half an hour and further reduced to 1/6 in 3 days. A list of the fission products selected in this study and their activities is presented in Table 4 in the

Appendix. They are calculated using elementary textbook physics and are assumed to arise from fissions of uranium-235 only.

This selection implies that radioactivity lasting only the first three days has been eliminated. This might be an improper assumption in the case of harbour accidents or groundings in very shallow waters. For sunken submarines at great depths in the Atlantic it is considered adequate.

The inventory has been calculated for a reactor operating period of 600 days at full power. After shut-down of the reactor the inventory will decay. The remaining activity is presented for decay periods of 3 days, 100 days and 1 000 days. During operation the inventory of short-lived isotopes reaches a saturation value depending on the half-life in question. This means that when the core lifetime is extended from 6 to 10 and now even to 15 years before replacement, the fission product inventory of short-lived isotopes does not increase correspondingly. Therefore, the bulk inventory stays constant, whereas the most unpleasant isotopes, the long-lived ones, increase steadily.

Radioactivity in primary system components

Surplus neutrons from the chain process in the core are absorbed in the major reactor components: the core support structure and the pressure tank and shielding. These components become radioactive. Corrosion products in the primary system and from the surface of the fuel cladding (crud) are also radioactive. The crud is deposited on the inner surface of pipeworks in the pressurizer, steamgenerator, valves and pumps. The total radioactivity level in these components is modest compared to the radioactivity of the reactor core.

Results of calculations made by the British National Radiological Protection Board of the activity level of solid components and crud for a 'generic' submarine one year after shutdown, are presented in Table 5 (ref. 20). Only those isotopes that contribute the most have been included here.

The term 'generic' implies that exact numbers cannot be given due to their being classified. In order to avoid the risk of disclosing design secrets, a 'generic' submarine is invented which is representative for the real thing. This is satisfactory for the public interest in the matter.

The halflives of the radioisotopes involved are relatively long. In fig. 31 the decay of activity of the dominant isotopes is shown.

Radionuclide	Halflife (years)	In solid components (Bq)	Primary circuit 'crud' (Bq)
Carbon-14	5 730	4.23×10^{11}	0.58×10^6
Iron-55	2.73	2.26×10^{15}	7.16×10^{10}
Cobalt-60	5.27	4.71×10^{14}	4.02×10^{12}
Nickel-59	7.5×10^4	1.73×10^{12}	5.07×10^7
Nickel-63	100.1	1.93×10^{14}	9.64×10^9
Total		2.93×10^{15}	4.10×10^{12}

Table 5 Radioactive inventories of plant components in a 'generic' submarine (Bq) (1 year after shutdown of reactor).

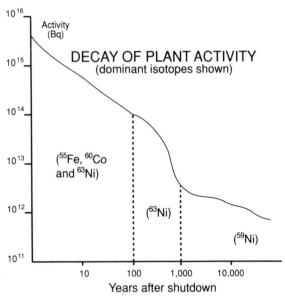

Fig. 31 The decay of the dominant radioactive isotopes in the components of a defuelled submarine reactor plant (logarithmic scale).

The build-up of plutonium in the core

Plutonium will be formed in any nuclear reactor core containing uranium-238. When uranium-238 absorbs a neutron it is eventually converted to an isotope of plutonium, plutonium-239 (how this element is formed is shown in the framed presentation). As the uranium fuel used in western nuclear submarines is enriched in uranium-235 to 97.3 percent, the remaining 2.7 percent uranium-238 gives a negligible amount of plutonium in the core.

Explanatory frame: The transuranics

Uranium is the element with the highest number of protons found in nature. The nuclear age has resulted in the artificial production of other elements with an even higher number of protons. They are labelled 'transuranics'. The most important ones in the present context are plutonium and americium.

Plutonium originates from uranium-238 by absorption of one neutron. This leads to uranium-239, which is unstable and so converts by emission of a beta-particle to neptunium-239 which is also unstable. With a half-life of 2.35 days neptunium-239 is converted to plutonium-239 by the emission of an additional beta-particle. Plutonium-239 has a half-life of 24 000 years.

Plutonium-239 will usually fission when absorbing a neutron, but not always: A certain fraction of the plutonium nuclei will, after the emission of gamma radiation, change into a plutonium-240 nucleus which is unstable with a half-life of 6 540 years. A further absorption of a neutron in plutonium-240 can lead to plutonium-241, and one more neutron to plutonium-242.

Plutonium-241 is radioactive with a half-life of 13.3 years. This means that over that much time half of the plutonium-241 isotopes will have been transformed to an isotope of another element, americium-241. Americium-241 is radioactive with a half-life of 440 years. It emits alpha and gamma radiation. 'Old' nuclear warheads containing plutonium need a cleaning operation to remove americium-241, because its radioactivity leads to irradiation of the staff handling the weapons during storage. One has to presume that the nuclear weapons in submarines are fresh due to the cramped space in the submarine.

All plutonium isotopes will be present in reactor cores which have been subject to high 'burn-ups' (subject to sustained exposure to neutron irradiation). However, the starting point is uranium-238. In submarine reactor cores with highly enriched uranium, 97.3 percent, there is only 2.7 percent uranium-238. The amount of plutonium in such cores will be negligible compared to the amounts in nuclear weapons. The uranium-235 isotopes either fission by absorption of a neutron, see frames on The Chain Process and The Fission Products, or they are transformed to the isotope uranium-236.

Soviet submarines do not use highly enriched uranium, at least not those of the Mike class. According to information from the Soviet Government in May 1989 in response to a questionnaire on the characteristics of the power plant of the Mike, this reactor is equipped with 'modestly enriched' fuel. Modest enrichment could be interpreted to be in the range of 30–50 percent or lower.

The plutonium content can be calculated if the enrichment level and fuel burn-up are known. No such calculations have been made for the purpose of this presentation. Adopting a pragmatic view, the plutonium content of a highly enriched submarine core could not be very different from the corresponding cores of highly enriched research reactors (except for the influence of unknown amounts of an unknown burnable poison). Fig. 32 shows the connection between enrichment and the net amount of plutonium produced in a research reactor per megawatt-day of energy release. This graph provides guidance for the International Atomic Energy Agency, IAEA, when they are assessing plutonium production in research reactors being safeguarded according to the Nuclear Proliferation Treaty, NPT.

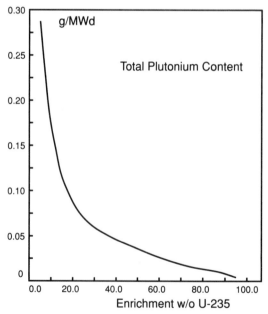

Fig. 32 Net plutonium content (grams/megawatt-day) in a fuel element versus enrichment.

It can be seen from the figure that an enrichment of 97.3 percent uranium-235 leads to almost no production of plutonium in the core. With an enrichment of 20 percent (arbitrarily chosen) the production rate is 0.075 grams per megawatt-day. For a 100 megawatt reactor operated for 600 days this means 0.075 x 100 x 600 grams equalling 4.5 kilograms of plutonium.

The Soviet authorities has revealed information on the content of plutonium, caesium-137 and strontium-90 in the core of the Mike:

Plutonium 2 kilograms
Cs-137   *$0.55x10^5$ Curie*   *($2.035x10^3$ TBq)*
Sr-90   *$0.42x10^5$Curie*   *($1.55x10^3$ TBq)*

There is a lack of internal consistency in these numbers. Comparing the value of Cs-137 with the corresponding one in Table 4 in the Appendix, it can be deduced that the Mike core has sustained a total energy release of about 16 900 megawatt-days. 2 000 grams of plutonium divided by 16 900 megawatt-days gives 0.12 grams per megawatt-day. Entering this value into fig. 32 one obtains an enrichment of about 11 percent. This is a little surprising since it indicates that the Mike core must be a rather conventional uranium-oxide core. (In contrast, the modern nuclear icebreakers use 90 percent enriched fuel.)

However, the simple interpretation above can be flawed. There is an added element of information hidden in the numbers given. If the energy release originated from uranium fissions alone, as in Table 4, the two fission products Cs-137 and Sr-90 should have been in about equal amounts as seen in Table 4. Fissions of plutonium-239, on the other hand, enhance the creation of Cs-137 relative to Sr-90. A large fraction of the fissions must have been due to plutonium, which is hard to understand with the low burnup. The ratio between the two isotopes seems to be too large to be explained in a simple way. Some sort of planted desinformation cannot be excluded.

Nuclear weapons in submarines

Nuclear weapons either contain uranium or plutonium of weapon grade at 93 percent or higher. The uranium weapons are, from a contamination point of view, of minor concern. Uranium will, if and when dispersed in the sea, mix with the uranium already there. The sea contains about 3 milligrams per cubic meter. Depending on its dispersion properties, however, plutonium will be harmful.

Plutonium in nuclear weapons

Modern nuclear weapons contain a mixture of uranium and plutonium. Most nuclear weapons onboard nuclear submarines are intercontinental strategic missiles containing multiple (MIRVed) warheads. The western Trident I C-4 missile with 8 warheads and the Soviet SS-N-20 Sturgeon also containing 7–10 warheads may serve as examples. The latter is a 3-stage solid fuel rocket.

It has been reported that the average content of plutonium in US nuclear weapons has been increased from about 2 kg to 4 kg per warhead, (ref. 21). Others quote the amount to be in the range of 3–7 kgs. The large intercontinental strategic weapons are thermo-nuclear. Plutonium is used in the 'trigger' part of the bomb, possibly about 4 kg per warhead. In addition, the trigger contains tritium which is essential to 'boost' or amplify the efficiency of the trigger charge. The amount of tritium necessary is 3–5 grams. Most of the energy released during the explosion derives from a fusion process involving tritium and deuterium. This tritium is, however, produced during the explosion itself. It does not exist in the warhead before the explosion.

The inventory of tritium in the weapons poses a radiation hazard if released into the environment. The health hazard of tritium is, however, low, so permissible release rates are accordingly high. Estimates of the amount of plutonium in a reactor core and in nuclear weapons are given in Table 6.

Source type	Total plutonium (kg)	TBq
Reactor fuel		
97.3%	negligible	
50.0%	1.8	5.2
20.0%	4.5	13
Nuclear warheads		
1 warhead	4.0	11.5
24 Trident I C-4 x 8 warheads	768	2.22×10^3

Table 6 Plutonium inventory in nuclear weapons and in a 100 megawatt reactor after 600 days of full operation.

Safety aspects of nuclear weapons

There are two safety issues of major importance related to the practical handling of nuclear weapons (ref. 22). The first one is to make the weapons as insensitive as possible to accidental triggering.

A warhead is usually constructed as a sphere of nuclear explosive, surrounded by a chemical explosive. The nuclear sphere is compressed when the chemical explosive detonates. This releases the nuclear reaction – the bomb explodes. The question is how to prevent ignition of the *nuclear* process if the chemical explosive should be ignited accidentally at a single point in the chemical explosive.

The chemical explosive is assembled as a number of cones. Each cone is ignited by a spark plug. A condition for 'controlled' ignition is that it takes place simultaneously in all cones so that the pressure wave created by the chemical explosion converges precisely towards the centre. Unless this happens, the whole weapon will be blown to pieces with no or very low release of nuclear energy.

The expression *one-point-safety* of a nuclear weapon means that the probability of *nuclear* ignition is negligible if accidental ignition takes place in a single cone of the chemical explosive.

The second safety issue relates to the reactivity of the chemical explosive itself. Even if a warhead is one-point-safe, an uncontrolled explosion might nevertheless lead to a spread of plutonium contaminating a large area. In 1959 two accidents occurred in Los Alamos, USA, during handling of the chemical high-explosive used in the tactical Sergeant ground-to-ground missile. The two accidents cost four lives, and uncovered a tendency of this particular chemical explosive to ignite unexpectedly. A new explosive, triamino-trinitro-benzene (TATB), was developed which was much less sensitive to external shocks. TATB can be shaped by tools (lathe) and will tolerate impacts of stray bullets without igniting. The explosive power of TATB, however, is lower than that of the high-explosive chemical. A consequence is therefore that a 'safe' warhead will need more fissile explosives for the same explosive yield. As part of the modernization process of US nuclear weapons, the old warheads are being replaced by new ones equipped with the insensitive chemical explosive. In 1984 about 1/3 of the warheads had been modernized.

Security aspects of nuclear weapons

Most American nuclear weapons are equipped with *electronic locks* (permissive action links, PAL) which will prevent a weapon being made ready for combat until a code authorization has been introduced. If anyone should attempt to circumvent PAL, the warhead is rendered useless after a few trials.

A correct signal for detonation could, in principle, be introduced by accident. To avoid this, many weapons have in addition a built-in sensor (ESD) which initiates detonation only after a pre-programmed ballistic orbit has been passed. The warhead cannot be misused should it be in unauthorized possession unless the code has been broken.

The security of nuclear weapons is greatly enhanced by these measures. The need for this is pretty obvious for weapons stored overseas and in potentially hostile areas where attempts to steal them could be expected. It is disappointing that this attitude of responsibility has not penetrated the US Navy. It has been reported that nuclear warheads in this navy are without these security measures, the reason apparently being that their weapons are better protected. It is not known what measures are being taken in other navies.

Missile propellants are concentrated sources of energy

Missiles carried onboard submarines may be propelled by either liquid or solid propulsion systems. Solid systems are generally preferred because they are easier to handle, store and use.

Liquid propulsion systems

Liquid propulsion systems have a liquid oxidizer (typically nitrogen tetraoxide, N_2O_4) and liquid fuel (hydrazine, unsymmetrical dimethylhydrazine or a mixture of the two). The fuel and oxidizer are stored in separate tanks on the missile and pumped to a nozzle (combustion chamber where they mix and ignite). The mixture is hypergolic – no ignition source is needed. The fuel and oxidizer may be stored in the missiles themselves or in storage tanks, with transfer to the missiles occurring prior to launch.

N_2O_4 boils at room temperature, and when it boils it evaporates as nitrogen dioxide NO_2, a noxious and toxic gas. Hydrazines are extremely reactive. If they spill or leak and come into contact with rusty metal, they will immediately burst into flame. A concurrent leak of hydrazine and N_2O_4 will result in an immediate fire. Such fires can be extinguished only by cutting off either the fuel or the oxidizer.

Solid propulsion systems

Solid rocket motors are powered by a solid propellant typically comprising a fuel (powdered aluminium), an oxidizer (ammonium perchlorate) and a rubber-like polymer binder to hold the fuel and oxidizer together. The binder may also serve as additional fuel.

Solid propulsion systems are inherently safe and stable with very limited potential for explosions. However, solid motors can be ignited by fires or sparks. Once ignited, they will burn at 2 000 to 4 000 °C until the propellant is spent.

5 Potential accidents with nuclear submarines

It is an unprecedented task to analyse potential accidents in nuclear submarines and their consequences. In the civilian nuclear power industry, a safety analysis starts within a framework of well-defined construction criteria and guidelines. The power plant is described in detail down to the last nut and bolt. The safety analysis comprises tens of thousands of pages describing any constellation of malfunctions of individual components. The results are presented as graphs showing probabilities of accidents which are so low that it is hard to imagine that an accident will ever happen.

An analysis of potential accidents in nuclear submarines can start at the other end. The accidents are so frequent that they can be described statistically. An independent safety analysis will suffer from having no access to construction criteria pertinent to nuclear submarines; no description of any nuclear submarine plant is available, and no design of the submarine is at hand in which the 'elusive' reactor is installed. The vulnerability of the reactor plant to external or internal accidents or shocks is not known and, finally, the submarine might sink anywhere with a wide spectrum of consequences.

Lacking precise information, one again has to turn to the civilian nuclear power industry, and make the best of it. The reactor systems are basically the same, the fission products are the same and, above all, the troublesome nuclear after-heat is definitely very much the same.

The troublesome nuclear after-heat

An oil-fired stove can be stopped immediately by cutting off the supply of oil – no after-heat is created. In a coal-fired stove after-heat will still be generated in the remaining coal if an oxygen supply is available.

When a nuclear reactor is stopped, no *new* fission products are created. Fission products already created will, however, continue to emit their individual radiation characteristics. This radiation is a heat source which decays in intensity with time and which needs cooling. The need for pumping power to provide cooling is most acute in the first hours and declines in the following days and weeks. If no pumps are operative, cooling can proceed by natural circulation processes only. If these processes are hampered by a faulty design, damage to the fuel elements cannot be avoided.

The time factors involved in the decay of nuclear after-heat are well known. The intensity depends on the reactor's mode of operation prior to sinking. Reactor cores with long operative service have the strongest after-heat. For a 100 megawatt plant, the after-heat will in practical terms yield about 2.2 megawatts after 10 minutes, 1.3 megawatts after 1 hour, 0.5 megawatts after 1 day and about 0.3 megawatts after 1 week. A number of short-lived fission products have decayed in a few days. Later the after-heat is due to the longer-lived isotopes which accordingly decays more slowly.

No safety assessment study of a nuclear submarine has been made public. However, the safety assessments of NS Otto Hahn, NS Savannah and, in general, the extensive US Reactor Safety Study, WASH-1400, which is an assessment of accident risks in US commercial nuclear power plants, and the corresponding Deutsche Risikostudie Kernkraftwerke (German Study of Nuclear Power Plant Risks) should serve the purpose.

There are certain safety features of submarine plants which deviate from the corresponding ones of landbased power plants. First, there are the increased risks in submarines of 'common mode failures'. Collisions, groundings or rocket propellant fires are common mode failures which can initiate a series of mishaps leading to a serious accident. There are presumably no parallels or the probabilities for such accidents are lower in landbased power stations.

All landbased PWR power plants are constructed with loop-type primary systems. The reactor pressure vessel is separated from the steam generators, pressurizer and pumps. An inherent weakness in this design is that the connecting pipelines can be broken, leading to what is known in the civilian nuclear industry as the Loss of Cooling Accident. The ultimate cooling of the core is dependent on an effective emergency core cooling system.

Several submarines are equipped with integrated primary systems where the steam generators, pressurizer and pumps are embedded within the pressure vessel. The Soviets seem to stick to loop systems, judging from their civilian ships. The British adhered to a loop design as well after careful evaluation. Integrated systems, however, have an advantage because the core volume is relatively small within the larger pressure vessel. This gives the primary system a higher heat capacity and might be helpful in stabilizing the heat transport out of the primary system.

Holes in the hull

The submarine pressure hull can be penetrated through collisions with other vessels. If the submarine is the striking vessel, it can be assumed that the outer hull will be an effective shock absorber. For Soviet submarines the pressure hull will be left intact, if at all affected.

If the submarine has a speed of 30 knots at the moment of collision (15 m/sec) and assuming that braking lasts for more than 1 second, the average braking deceleration will remain lower than 1.5 g (g is the acceleration of gravity). The design values for the reactor plant itself and for the plant's cradle are expected to be higher than this. No damage to the reactor plant is therefore anticipated.

If a Soviet submarine (with a double hull) is struck by another vessel, the outer hull will provide good protection. The colliding ship will penetrate the submarine to a greater or lesser extent. Deformation and destruction in the impact zones absorb a considerable amount of energy and the acceleration is rapidly reduced. The deceleration created might have repercussions throughout the length of both ships. The lateral displacement of the submarine will be slight, with some heeling. The deceleration forces are not expected to damage the reactor plant. There is, however, a possibility that the pressure hull may be punctured, leading to the sinking of the submarine. Thanks to their two parallel independent pressure hulls, the larger Soviet submarines will probably not sink.

An extensive series of collision experiments has been performed at GKSS-Forschungssentrum Geesthacht GMBH in the Federal Republic of Germany. The experiments were part of the development programme for nuclear-propelled cargo ships. The objective was to design an adequate shield around the reactor plant in order to protect it against collisions. It was demonstrated that a mechanical web-like structure occupying the space between the reactor and the penetrating bow was well suited to absorb the collision energy. The nuclear plant in the larger Soviet submarines with double hulls is therefore well protected. Submarines with just one hull (all the Western submarines) are more vulnerable.

Fires and explosions

Fires and related explosions constitute the most frequent accidents in Soviet submarines. To which extent this is the case for Western submarines is not well known. Arkin et al. (ref. 23) have shed more light on this.

A fire might start from a short-circuit in electrical cables. This was said to be the cause of the fire in the Soviet submarine Mike which sank in the North Atlantic in April 1989. The fire spread swiftly from compartment to compartment. Explosions followed and the submarine sank.

If the fourth of the barriers protecting the environment against the radioactive contents of the reactor, the hull, has been broken down, the submarine sinks. What about the third barrier, the containment structure? Explosions which puncture the submarine hull might have destroyed the containment structure as well. Trapped air pockets containing oil can explode if compressed sufficiently during sinking. The butterfly valves ensuring flooding of the containment with sea water during sinking, but which close again when the vessel rests on the seabed, might be destroyed by an explosion. Damage to welding seams in the containment structure is also possible. If so, the third barrier is broken.

The second barrier, the reactor primary system, would probably not be mechanically ruptured by an explosion outside the containment. Integrated system designs are very compact. In a loop system the pipes between the pressure vessel and the steam-generators may rupture, leading to an accident scenario like the one described later on. If so, the second barrier is broken and will no longer afford protection.

The first barrier, the fuel elements with their claddings, is unlikely to be broken down by a mechanical shock, however violent, if properly designed. All the 10 000–15 000 fuel pins, if that is the design, are individually isolated from the reactor primary system. Single pins might crack, releasing part of their radioactive content to the reactor primary system. A major breakdown of this (multiple) barrier can only come about if another failure, like loss of cooling, should lead to a substantial temperature increase which melts all or a considerable part of the claddings. Fuel of plate design is probably close to shock-proof.

A violent mechanical shock is an initiating mechanism for common mode failures, but the direct impact on the plant's integrity would most likely be on other parts of the plant than the reactor fuel. The free mobility of control rods in and out of the core presupposes a very rigid mechanical design of the rods and their guide tubes. If guide tubes are bent as a result of an explosion, some control rods might stick and it might be more difficult to stop the reactor.

Fires and explosions might lead to the steam turbine being 'tripped', i.e. stopped. If this occurs without the reactor being completely stopped simultaneously, the fuel will become overheated. If the emergency core cooling then also fails, a dangerous situation with potential releases will occur.

An accident scenario involving loss of emergency core-cooling pumping power

Dr. G. Finke in his doctoral thesis (ref. 24) has performed a theoretical analysis of a projected civilian nuclear-propelled ship that sinks. The propulsion plant studied provided 220 megawatts of thermal power and had an integrated primary system. When the ship sank, it was assumed that the emergency core-cooling system failed due to the loss of pumping power, and the question was how the nuclear after-heat was dealt with. The nuclear after-heat calculated was 8 megawatts 1 minute after shut-down of the reactor, 4.1 megawatts after 16 minutes and 1 megawatt after 30 hours.

The tilting of the ship as it rests on the seabed, i.e. the angle to the vertical assumed by the fuel elements, is relevant for the subsequent cooling of the reactor core.

In Dr. Finke's analysis it was presumed that the primary system remained sealed, that the containment had been filled with sea water during sinking and that the valves isolating the containment were closed when pressures inside and outside the containment walls were equalized. It was further assumed that the containment was cooled from the outside by free circulating sea water.

Heat transport out of the core

The after-heat must be removed by a cooling process, but how? If the heat is not removed, the heat energy released by the fission products will build up and the temperature of the fuel elements will increase. The rate of temperature increase will depend on the heat-absorbing capacities of the coolant and the fuel, as well as the construction materials. By heat capacity is meant the energy absorbed necessary to increase the temperature by 1 degree centigrade. A reactor designer knows these numbers well. Heat capacities for submarine cores are not known.

In the absence of pumping power, free convection circulation is the only means to bring the heat out of the core. Heat from the fuel is absorbed by the water in the primary system. Its further removal, however, is arrested since the normal heat sink, the secondary system with steam turbines and condenser, does not function. Two mechanisms remain for removing the heat from the primary system. Firstly, steam can be blown off through the steam safety valves. This happens when the internal pressure exceeds pre-set limits over and above outside pressure. This pressure will depend on the depth of the seabed. Secondly, heat can be removed through direct cooling of the pressure vessel by sea water in the flooded containment.

Melting of the core

Dr. Finke presumed that the ship sin! to shallow depths, 200 meters, only. As long as the heat removed directly by conduction through the pressure vessel wall is less than the after-heat input, the safety valve will continue to blow off steam until the pressures are equalized. The water level within the pressure vessel might sink below the upper edge of the reactor core. The upper part of the hot fuel is then not effectively cooled, and the temperature of this part of the core increases considerably. The heat is then transferred to the pressure vessel wall in two different ways: 1) direct heat transport to the wall through the remaining water (as before), and 2) a new effect, i.e. thermal radiation from the exposed core.

A new heat source arises if and when the temperature of the cladding (if this is zircaloy) reaches a level where the cladding reacts chemically with the water. The cladding oxidises to zirconium-oxide with the simultaneous release of hydrogen gas and energy (heat). The temperature and pressure of the primary system increase further. Submarine fuel is probably clad mainly with stainless steel.

Dr. Finke describes how the increased temperature, for a given set of assumptions, ultimately initiates the melting of the core so that 60 percent of the core will melt in 19.6 days. The molten fuel falls into the remaining water. No violent fuel-water explosion is anticipated, as the fuel is not divided into sufficiently fine particles. The reactor pressure-vessel tank wall will not melt. It is cooled from the outside by the containment water and its integrity remains intact.

The tilting angle has a pronounced effect on the whole cooling sequence. As the angle increases, heat removal decreases. A sample calculation shows that in a vertical position, 2.4 megawatts of after-heat will be removed by conduction and 0.9 megawatts by thermal radiation. These figures are reduced to 0.4 and 0.28 megawatts, respectively, at a tilting angle of 85 degrees.

The sunken Soviet submarine Mike has been observed resting on the seabed in an upright position, according to an announcement from the Soviet Union. No such information is available about the other sunken submarines.

One should not draw too far-reaching conclusions from this sample calculation. The plant studied had a power level which was twice that of most of the submarine plants in operation. The example just shows that the possibility of partial melting cannot be ignored.

It is apparent that if the propulsion plant sinks to much larger depths, 2 000–3 000 meters or more, the cooling sequence will be different. No analysis of this case has been made, however. The safety valves have to let off the steam against increased external sea water pressure. With a safety-valve release pressure of 121 bars, and a depth of 1 000 meters, (100 bars), the internal pressure has to rise to 221 bars before the safety valves will open. This corresponds to a temperature of 374 °C. The fuel will then be cooled by superheated steam. The thermal stresses in the tank wall will be considerable. In addition, water at high temperatures is very corrosive.

An accident scenario involving loss of coolant (LOCA)

Loss of coolant can be a serious problem since it implies a breakdown of the primary system. There is a wide spectrum of processes leading to loss of coolant; from small breaks to large breaks. Safety studies on civilian PWR plants identify the 'double-ended guillotine break of a cold leg pipe close to the pressure vessel' as a maximum limiting event against which the safety systems are designed and their performances analyzed. This type of accident can only take place in reactors with loop-type (dispersed) primary system designs.

How a LOCA can develop

During a LOCA, the primary system coolant water is rapidly expelled from the pressure vessel. This 'blow-down' phase takes about half a minute. The loss of reactor pressure will initiate the insertion of reactor control rods, causing the chain reaction to cease immediately. The after-heat in the fuel decays steadily but during the hours that follows it will be several megawatts.

Partial cooling can be obtained for a limited time if pressurized accumulators discharge coolant water into the core. It is not known whether submarine plants have such accumulators. About a quarter of an hour after the accident started, the primary system water has boiled off and overheating of the core will begin.

The further development of the accident depends on whether the submarine is floating or whether she sinks. If the submarine is afloat, it further depends on whether emergency power – a second reactor, batteries or diesel engines – can provide pumping power for the emergency core cooling system. If the submarine sinks, the extent of the damage to the core depends on how long it takes before the containment and the reactor core become flooded by sea water. Inflowing seawater will cool the core efficiently and prevent melting. If so, corrosion of the cladding by sea-water will be the next threat to the environment.

The June 1989 accident in the Norwegian Sea with an Echo II class submarine is an example of a small-break LOCA-type accident, based on the official information from the Soviet authorities. While the submarine was submerged, a leak developed in the primary system (by no means comparable to a 'Maximum Credible Accident'). The submarine surfaced and both reactors were shut down, see fig. 5. Nothing has been revealed about why the second reactor was shut down. Emergency diesel engines were started. The steam escaping was led to a water-filled 'bubbling tank' for condensation, indicating that the reactor is equipped with a pressure suppression system. The radiation level was reported to be slight, which would mean that no damage had occurred to the fuel. The supply of fresh water onboard was considered insuffi-

Fig. 33 The picture shows the supply of emergency cooling water to the Echo II submarine during the accident in the Norwegian Sea June 28, 1989.

cient to cool down the reactor, and therefore fresh water was supplied by assisting Soviet tankers, see fig. 33. The air conditioners ceased to operate. Members of the crew were observed on deck in life-jackets. Understandably, the steam in the containment must have made the indoor environment too hot for the crew.

The Soviet authorities have maintained that no radioactive material was released into the environment as a result of this accident. This is not quite true. Radioactive iodine-131 and lanthanides were recorded in both air and water samples. The radioactivity level of the primary coolant water is never zero. The radioactivity of the water stems from three processes. Firstly, there might be leaky fuel pins. Secondly, during production of the fuel pins, it is inevitable that the surface of the cladding will be slightly contaminated by dust particles of uranium. Fission products from this dust are dissolved by the water. Thirdly, rust particles from the construction materials in the steel pressure vessel, piping etc. ('crud') are irradiated in the reactor and become radioactive. The containment and reactor primary system must have been severely contaminated.

Normally all this radioactive material is continuously removed from the coolant water by shielded filters. If the radioactivity level of the coolant water becomes too high, the crew will be exposed to overdoses of irradiation from the reactor plant and the core will then normally have to be replaced. It is not known at what level of radiation refuelling is required. In the Soviet civilian power stations, the maximum permissible specific activity of non-gaseous fission products in the coolant water 2 hours after sampling is 3.7×10^8 Bq (becquerels) per liter of water. If it is (arbitrarily) assumed that 10 tons of such water had escaped the pressure system, 3.7 TBq (tera-becquerels, tera $= 10^{12}$) would have been released to the containment. If the containment was leaky, this would be most unpleasant for the crew, in particular the effects of the iodine-131 isotope. A clean-up and repair operation would be difficult. In view of the age of the Echo II class submarine, this unit will most probably be withdrawn from active service.

Experimental simulations of LOCAs
In assessing the safety of nuclear plants, whether civilian or not, it is of vital interest to be able to determine experimentally what would happen if a reactor core is deprived of cooling. How long will it take before the temperature has increased to such a level that the cladding is

destroyed, and how much longer before the fuel melts? A considerable amount of theoretical and experimental development work has been performed to establish criteria for emergency core cooling. In the USA a special reactor, the Loss of Coolant Test Facility (LOFT) in Idaho, was constructed for this purpose. The reactor operates at a power level of 55 megawatts. The British DS/MP reactor at Dounreay has, after completion of its service as a prototype for the PWR 1 reactor, been converted to a test plant for loss-of-coolant experiments.

In 1985 an experiment was conducted in LOFT to verify the validity of recent studies and computer programmes on what fractions of fission products (Source Terms) would be released if fuel elements are severely damaged. In order to simulate a Three Mile Island type accident, a 'small-to-intermediate-size' break was initiated in the LOFT primary coolant system, the reactor was stopped, the core drained of water and the delivery of emergency coolant was deliberately delayed.

After about 12 1/2 minutes the uncovered core began to heat up. After approximately 24 minutes the temperature in a 100-pin insulated experimental fuel element reached 1800 °C, and the oxidation of fuel-pin zircaloy cladding began. This oxidation released still more energy and drove the temperature up to more than 2200 °C. For approximately four and a half minutes a test bundle of 11 fuel pins was purposely deprived of cooling water. This caused the cladding and fuel to melt and the radioactive fission products were released within the reactor. Emergency core cooling was then initiated to terminate the experiment. Within 15 seconds the fuel was cooled down (ref. 25).

The LOFT series of experiments supports the belief that the time margins in the case of a LOCA are sufficient to achieve adequate cooling of the core, if the submarine sinks and the containment and primary system are flooded. If the submarine does not sink, no flooding occurs and the submarine has its emergency power sources operative, one has to assume that the propulsion plant is designed to supply sufficient emergency coolant to the core. If these power sources fail, the core will inevitably melt.

The nuclear submarines already resting on the seabed

Three of the sunken submarines, the USS Thresher, USS Scorpion and the Soviet Mike have been located, identified and photographed.

Their localizations are shown in fig. 41. Thresher is resting at a depth of 2 500 meters, Scorpion at 3 100 meters and Mike at 1 685 meters.

Thresher is heavily damaged. Debris is scattered over an area of several square kilometers. It is not possible from the published pictures to judge anything about potential damage to the nuclear plant. However, the Thresher had just undergone an extensive overhaul, possibly including renewal of the reactor core. If so, the fission product content of the core will be so low as to render the submarine completely harmless.

The debris from the Scorpion is also scattered over a large area. The hull is compressed from the ends. It is not possible to judge the conditions at the reactor compartment.

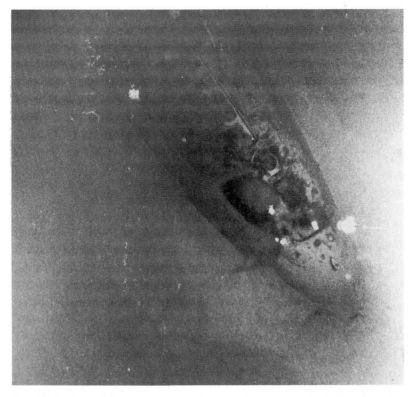

Fig. 34 A view of the bow section of the nuclear-powered attack submarine USS Scorpion (SSN-589) where it rests on the bottom of the ocean 400 miles southwest of the Azores Islands.

Fig. 35 An overview of the large, hatch-like opening located on the aft section of the USS Scorpion, where the messenger buoy is stowed. A mooring line is protruding from its stowage locker into the messenger buoy cavity. Other objects clearly visible are the circular main ballast tank vents, two rectangular hatches into the superstructure and damaged snorkel exhaust piping.

A video tape of the Soviet Mike has been made available to the scientific community in the west by the Soviets. The video shows apparent heat damage to the outer hull – supporting testimonies of the survivors that internal explosions took place. Some crew hatches are open. The thickness of the titanium hull can be seen together with the spacing between the outer and inner hulls.

The stern section is missing. This could be due to damage to the hull during the fire and strong bending forces during the sinking. The submarine has apparently hit the bottom with enough force to push debris out for several meters. A lot of damage to the vessel could have arisen during the sinking and on impact with the bottom. One might speculate, however, that the soft boundary layer has dampened the shock of hitting the bottom sufficient to keep accelerations within design values and that the propulsion plant therefore may be intact.

Fig. 36 is an identification of the Mike. The number read, 1989, could be a datum or a pennant number? It is not possible to judge conditions at the propulsion plant.

The seabed around the debris of Thresher and Scorpion has been investigated three times so far. Samples show minor amounts of cobalt-

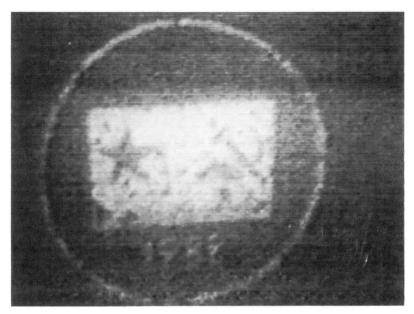

Fig. 36 Identification of the sunken Soviet nuclear submarine Mike.

60, indicating leakage from the reactor primary system. The dose level close to Mike has been recorded to be 20 mikro-roentgens (0.2 mikro-Sieverts) per hour. This compares with the recorded activity level of 5 micro-Sieverts per hour on the top of the empty, defuelled British submarine Dreadnaught. The latter, however, is not shielded by sea water.

Release of radioactive material

An important problem is: how much of the total fission product inventory in the reactor core, as given in Table 4 (see Appendix), can be released to the environment after an accident?

'Source Terms' for the release of radioactive substances from a reactor

The 'Source Terms' express the *relative* amounts of the various fission products released as fractions of their core inventories at the start of the accident. Furthermore, the Source Terms denote the release char-

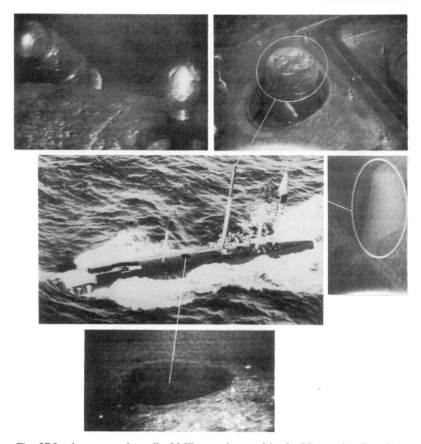

Fig. 37 In the centre the sail of Mike as observed in the Norwegian Sea. Surrounding this picture are presented stills taken from a video taken by the Soviet Navy. Some of the masts are identified. The conical top to the right is a satellite navigation antenna with the NATO code name Pert Spring.

acteristics, consisting of such information as the energy content, timing and duration of the release.

Substantial information on the Source Terms is, in fact, available for civilian nuclear fuel. These Source Terms are specific for the fuel pin design and their properties. Detailed knowledge of submarine fuel and plant design is, therefore, essential for applying this information properly to the submarine. For the crossing of each barrier the consequential release has to be considered.

In order to predict the probable release of fission products from the fuel matrix to the internal fuel gap, the build-up of the Source Terms can be divided into three broad regimes (ref. 26).

The first regime concerns the release from the fuel matrix into the free volume of the pin during normal operation. This portion of released material is known as the 'gap inventory'. The amount of each fission product present in the pin voidage depends on the irradiation conditions of the pin prior to the accident. The total core inventory of these fission products is given in Table 4, see Appendix. The fraction of these products which constitutes the gap inventory for normal operating temperatures up to 1 300 °C is given in Table 7. The figures, which are considered to be rather conservative and are valid for uranium oxide fuel, are based upon a large amount of experimental evidence (ref. 26).

The second regime covers temperatures greater than 1 200 °C which may arise as a result of an accident. Then the release of fission products from the fuel starts to become important as the temperature rises towards 1 800 °C (the melting point of zirconium cladding), see Table 8. The release of very large fractions of the total inventory of the more volatile fission products can be expected.

The third regime covers temperatures greater than 1 800 °C. Meltdown of fuel and cladding will then start.

Fission product	Gap inventory (fraction of total core inventory) (1)	Gap release (fraction of gap inventory) (2)	Release (fraction of total core inventory) (1) x (2)
Xenon-Krypton	0.005	1.0	0.005
Iodine-Bromine	0.005	1.0	.005
Caesium-Rubidium	0.005	1.0	.005
Tellur-Selen-Antimon	0.005	10^{-3}	5×10^{-6}
Strontium-Barium	0.005	10^{-4}	5×10^{-7}
UO$_2$ dust			5×10^{-4}

Table 7 Fission product gap inventories and release at temperatures up to 1 300 °C, civilian fuel.

Fission	Release fractions of total core inventory at: (°C)					
product	1 300	1 400	1 500	1 600	1 700	1 800
Inert gases	0.10	0.24	0.44	0.70	0.93	1.0
Iodine-Bromine	0.10	0.24	0.44	0.70	0.93	1.0
Caesium-Rubidium	0.10	0.24	0.44	0.70	0.93	1.0
Tellur-Selen	2×10^{-4}	8×10^{-4}	3×10^{-3}	0.012	0.047	0.17
Antimon				0.002	0.007	0.03
Molybdenum				0.0015	0.006	0.023
Ba, Sr, Tc, Ru,		negligible				
Rh, Pd, Rare Earths		negl.				
Zr		negl.				

Table 8 Additional thermal release in temperature range 1 300 °C to 1 800 °C after release of gap inventory, exposure time 10 minutes.

The release of inert gases and volatile fission products from the fuel matrix into the fuel gap is very temperature-dependent in the range 1 000 °C to 2 000 °C. Below this range, release is essentially dependent on fuel rating (watts per cm) and surface area and is controlled by thermal diffusion processes. These processes result in release levels of one or two tenths of one percent and increase slowly with fuel burn-up.

Noble gases and volatile isotopes like caesium and iodine are increasingly released to the gap if the fuel temperature increases up to 1 800 °C. Low fuel burn-ups tend to reduce the releases. It seems prudent to assume that for temperatures exceeding 1 600 °C and for overheatings lasting longer than 10 minutes, the predicted release of all volatile products is close to 100 percent (ref. 26, p 473). However, the release of the more volatile isotopes is expected to be complete within a few minutes at temperatures greater than 2 000 °C (ref. 26).

One way to reduce the temperature effect and thereby reduce the fission gas release into the fuel pin voidage could be to reduce the fuel pin diameter. More pins would then have to be accommodated within a fuel element. For unchanged fuel-element power level, this would result in a significant decrease in individual pin power. The rise in temperature from surface to centre of a fuel pin is directly proportional to the linear heat rating (watts cm^{-1}).

Present-day civilian PWR fuel designs have peak linear heat ratings of the order of 300 watts cm^{-1} and fuel centre temperature in the region of 1 100 °C or less. For uranium oxide fuel the centre temperature as a function of linear heat rating was shown in fig. 18. This relationship is independent of pin diameter.

It should again be stressed that the Source Terms given in Tables 9 and 10 are valid for uranium oxide fuel pins. Submarine fuel designs using another matrix and geometrical shape will have different Source Terms, although releases of inert gases and volatile fission products could be very much the same. The values of the Source Terms are continuously being revised as new experimental evidence with improved fuel designs is made available.

If the cladding is sufficiently oxidized, it might be embrittled to the extent that it could fragment when subjected to thermal shock forces generated in the abrupt cooling (quench) during reflooding of the core, or in the event of other mechanical shocks. Criteria for the onset of embrittlement of the cladding due to extensive oxidation have been established. One of them is that the calculated maximum fuel element cladding temperature should not exceed 1 200 °C at any time (ref. 26). When the zircaloy cladding temperature exceeds 1 850–1 950 °C the zircaloy melts and the fuel matrix is left exposed.

The use of zircaloy as cladding in submarine cores is probably very limited. The alternative would be stainless steel. Data on the oxidation of stainless steel(304) with steam at high temperatures is sparse. The results tend to show that the reaction is slower than the oxidation of zircaloy at temperatures below 1 150 °C, but faster at temperatures greater than 1 150 °C. At 1 400 °C and above, the steel foams during oxidation.

The potential release to the reactor primary system

When applying the Source Terms given in Tables 9 and 10 to the fission product inventory in a 100 megawatt submarine reactor, one would obtain the release to the reactor primary system if there should be a complete break-down of the first barrier, the fuel cladding. Since the first barrier consists of 10 000 to 15 000 individual sub-barriers, such a release can only come about if there is a common cause for the destruction of the claddings, i.e. very high temperature. Table 9 should be interpreted in this context. Even so, the fraction released is only about 12 percent for the maximum temperature (1 800 °C) considered.

Fission product (1)	Core invent. 10^4 TBq (2)	Fraction released 1 300 °C 10^4 TBq (3)	Added release 1 800 °C 10^4 TBq (4)	Total release 1 800 °C 10^4 TBq (5) = (4)+(3)
Xe-Kr	15.7	0.0785	15.6	15.7
I-Br	7.5	0.0375	7.4	7.5
Cs-Rb	1.7	0.0085	1.7	1.7
Te-Se- Sb	10.6	0.053×10^{-3}	1.8	1.8
Sr-Ba	32.3	0.016×10^{-3}	–	0.016×10^{-3}
Mo	8.5		0.2	0.2
Others	157	0.0785	–	78.5×10^{-3}
Sum	223.3	0.203	26.7	27

Table 9 The core inventory of fission products in a 100-megawatt reactor core operated for 600 days, 3 days after the shut-down of the reactor, together with potential releases to the reactor primary system in the case of a complete breakdown of all fuel element claddings. Unit of radioactivity is TBq (tera-becquerel, tera = 10^{12}).

Fission product retention in the primary system

To what extent may fission products which have been released from the fuel pins be retained in the primary system even if the system is leaky? The processes involved are very complex, but there seem to be three retaining mechanisms (ref. 26). These are:

– hold-up in any water retained in the system
– settling and adhesion of particulates
– plating, i.e. the condensation of volatiles into surfaces, physisorption, chemisorption and chemical interaction with penetration of the surface

When depressurization of the primary systems starts, the steam generated will carry over a very small portion of fission products from the coolant. The steam generated will condense quickly in the bubbling tanks if the containment is sealed, or in the intruding sea water.

The inert gases xenon and krypton have a low solubility in water and will be released completely from a ruptured primary system. Iodine is probably carried from the core predominantly as iodide ions, formed from caesium iodide released from the core. The retention of the other fission products in the primary system water might be considerable, but it is prudent to assume that the amount carried to the containment structure will simply be proportional to the amount of primary water transferred and that this amount will be 100 percent.

The second process by which radioactive substances can be retained in the primary system is settling and adhesion of particulates. Particulates are usually insoluble in water and would consist predominantly of fuel debris or oxidised cladding. The deposition processes are, however, not efficient. Therefore, no credit should be taken for retention.

Plating processes like physisorption and chemisorption can remove a significant amount of activity from the coolant water. Iodine is the fission product for which evidence of plating from the coolant is available. However, in the case of physisorption, plated material will be re-released to the coolant water as soon as the concentration of dissolved fission products falls. No retention of fission products on the walls of the primary system can therefore be assumed in the presence of a liquid coolant.

In summary, it is a conservative assumption that the Source Terms to the containment structure will be identical to the release from the reactor fuel to the reactor primary system. Depending on the specifics of the damage from the accident and the circulation rate of coolant (sea) water, a certain hold-up time of the fission products contained in the water in the submarine can be expected. The driving force for the circulation rate will be the after-heat in the fuel.

Retention of fission products in the reactor containment

The fission products and other radioactive substances entering the containment structure might be retained by the same processes as those valid for the primary system. The containment will be filled with sea water, with the exception of possible pockets of trapped air also containing aerosols. The same arguments can be applied for the retention processes in the containment as for those in the primary system. The conclusion will be that, except for a delaying effect, no faith can be placed in any lasting retention of radioactive substances. The release to the marine environment must therefore be assumed to be identical to the release to the primary system, Table 9.

The break-down of safety barriers due to corrosion in sea water

Sealed barriers might break down due to corrosion in sea water. Interest has been focused on the corrosion aspects in connection with a proposed dumping of the defuelled, decommissioned British submarine Dreadnought in the Atlantic (ref. 20). Actual rates of corrosion of ordinary and stainless steel have been taken from that reference and are shown in Table 10. The presence of oxygen in the sea water is a pre-condition for corrosion. At great depths the oxygen content is lower than in shallow waters. The corrosion rate at such depths will therefore be correspondingly lower. Fuel claddings will be kept warm due to the nuclear afterheat and the corrosion-active sea water will rise in temperature. The rates of corrosion of the cladding will then be (slightly) higher.

Type of steel	Corrosion mechanism	Corrosion rate (m y^{-1})
ordinary	pitting	$1.10^{-5} - 7.10^{-5}$
ordinary	bulk corrosion	$6.10^{-6} - 1.5.10^{-4}$
stainless	pitting	$2.10^{-4} - 4.10^{-4}$
stainless	bulk corrosion	$3.10^{-9} - 2.10^{-5}$

Table 10 Rates of corrosion of ordinary and stainless steel in sea water.

The bulk corrosion (corrosion attacking the full surface) of an (assumed) 2 centimeter thick containment ordinary steel wall, the third barrier, will in oxygen-rich water take from 100–200 years upwards. An (assumed) 7 cm thick pressure vessel wall, the second barrier, might stay sealed for 1000 years or more, taking into account rates of corrosion only. The presence of ordinary low-grade steel within the hull will provide anodic protection of the stainless steel components. The weakest points, however, could be gaskets and sealed penetrations through the main steel body for instrument cablings.

The first barrier, the stainless steel cladding, is arbitrarily assumed to be 0.3 mm. It could be thicker, but hardly thinner. Cladding materials used by the US Navy are subject to a corrosion rate of 'a few millionths of an inch per year' ($\sim 10^{-7}$ my^{-1}) in sea water. If so, the cladding lasts a few thousand years. This corrosion will start only after the second barrier has been penetrated and it presumes that oxygen is present in the sea water. The cladding is also corroded from the inside by the fission products.

Part three

– and the potential environmental impact

Part three reflects on the potential environmental impact of a sunken nuclear submarine. No sunken submarine has reportedly so far released significant amounts of radioactive material. The fission products contained in the nuclear plant decay with time. When the protective barriers have been broken down by corrosion the remaining long-lived fission products will leak. The next sunken nuclear submarine might, however, leak from the very beginning. The potential consequences should be considered in advance. They will not necessarily be dramatic; that will depend on the extent of damage to the nuclear plant, where the accident has taken place and on the conditions for dispersal by ocean currents. An accident involving large releases of radioactive material in a shallow coastal region with high biological production could, however, have serious consequences for the marine species in that region and be a disaster for the fishing industry of the region.

6 Environmental impact of a sunken nuclear submarine

The inventory of radioactive products in a sunken nuclear submarine, if released into the environment under unfavourable conditions, can constitute a potential threat to marine species and to man. The magnitude of this threat will depend on where the submarine rests and, obviously, on the extent of leakage. If there is no release, no harm will be done.

The threat, however, has two components. The first is due to the fission products. If the reactor remains sealed for a couple of centuries, the problem decays along with the dying fission products. Break-down due to corrosion of the barriers surrounding the fission products might pave the way for releases. The second component is the plutonium in (primarily) any nuclear weapons onboard. That threat lasts forever.

Submarines located on the deep-sea seabeds are far less threatening than submarines in shallow waters with high biological production. The six sunken submarines in the Atlantic Ocean and the Barents Sea are resting at 2 000–3 000 meters depth and they are sealed, so why bother? The authorities responsible should document the rationale for not bothering. The public has good reason not to be impressed by general statements about the safety of nuclear submarines. Statistics predict that the seventh will join the others within five years. Where? Can anyone guarantee that it will be in the deep seas?

Impact on marine species and the pathway to man

An analysis of the threat of a sunken submarine in shallow waters should, in principle, include the study of all potential pathways of radioactive products to man and of the impacts on marine species. The pathways can be thoroughly assessed if suitable theoretical models for the sea dispersion of these products are available, and if more fundamental knowledge on the uptake of radioactive materials and responses to radiation exposures are obtained. The analysis will need to determine whether and how upper limits are reached on a permissible intake of contaminated food by man in accordance with the limits recommended by The International Commission for Radiological Protection and it will also need to determine the burden on fish populations and marine ecosystems. This is the normal practice in cases of approved, limited releases of radioactive products into the environment. A sunken nuclear submarine, however, is not a normal event for which normal procedures apply.

The mass media will make it abundantly clear that no radioactive marine food from the infected area should be consumed. No immediate harm to the public is therefore impending. The long term effects of the contamination might, however, be of importance. Political effects on the fishing industry could be disastrous, irrespective of the actual risks involved. These risks should therefore be investigated thoroughly and honestly.

The important point is to which extent contamination of sea food (fish, shellfish, molluscs etc.) has taken place or will take place, its distribution and its duration. The impact on marine species consists of effects in contaminated individuals, populations and ecosystems. A complete survey of these effects would entail (ref. 27):

a. Quantifying radioactive sources including the natural background, releases from the civilian nuclear power industry, nuclear weapons accidents and leakages from sunken nuclear submarines
b. Determining distributions of radioactivity in the environment and recognition of their dynamic variations both in space and time
c. Determining the biochemical and geochemical transfer mechanisms and factors during transport from source to uptake
d. Computing radiation dose rates
e. Establishing responses to radiation exposure
f. Recognizing acceptability of effects, value judgement

A total evaluation of the consequences for the environment of sunken nuclear submarines in the North Atlantic is beyond the scope of this book. The main focus here has been on quantifying the source (a) and on examining aspects of the dispersion problem (b). These aspects include a description of the most relevant oceanographic processes pertinent to deep sea contaminant transport and for modelling the dispersion. The general description is illustrated by examples of other (known) releases to the environment. Such releases either take place under controlled conditions, like the dumping of radioactive waste in the Atlantic and the releases of waste to the sea from nuclear reprocessing plants, or they imply the spread of nuclear debris from nuclear weapons accidents. The other points above (c-e) will be dealt with in a cursory manner only.

There are limitations to this method of presentation. Each sunken submarine is a potential source of radioactive pollutants. The pollutants will disperse in the environment from the source in a way which is specific for the particular location. Dispersion will depend on depth, sea-bed structure and prevailing deep sea currents. Some regions on the seabed are relatively calm. In other places the 'sea weather' might be rather stormy. The Soviets have reported difficulties in getting close to the sunken Mike submarine with submersibles due to strong currents. One submersible got a damaged propeller in a collision with the wreck. However, the cause could be sea currents acting on the supporting cables.

Knowledge of the characteristics of one source point cannot be used to evaluate the consequences of dispersion from another arbitrary source point. However, at any time a nuclear submarine may sink right on an established dumping site for radioactive waste where radioactive effluents have been seeping out for many years. If so, the consequences of releases at these sites has already been thoroughly analyzed and it is interesting to compare releases of the same type of nuclides. This may give some indications as to the order of magnitude of the effects, under most favourable circumstances.

Knowledge of the dispersion alone is not sufficient to assess potential consequences. The uptake of radioactive materials in marine species and the pathways to man is also site-specific and has to be established. This uncertainty in the assessment of the true consequences of a sunken submarine points to the need for improved models describing the dispersion of effluents in the sea.

Considering the substantial concentration of nuclear propelled ships in the Barents Sea and the prospective oil-drilling activities there, the probability of a major accident involving nuclear submarines and oil leakages is anything but negligible. A collision has already occurred between a German (non-nuclear) submarine and an oil-rig in the North Sea. A minimum of preparedness would be to develop a dispersion model for the Barents Sea which can predict where the pollutants most likely will flow.

Reference concentration levels of radioactivity in the sea and marine systems

A sub-task of quantifying the source level of a sunken nuclear submarine is to establish reference levels of radioactivity in the sea in advance of an accident. The reference level is due to naturally radioactive substances as well as man-made radioactivity from fall-out from nuclear weapons testing and effluents from nuclear reprocessing plants. The impact of potential releases from a sunken nuclear submarine with a distribution as predicted from dispersion models could then be compared to the actual levels of radioactivity observed in the North Sea, the Norwegian Sea and in the Barents Sea.

Natural background radioactivity in sea water
More than 60 nuclides are naturally radioactive. The most important ones found in the sea are presented in Table 11, see Appendix, while a more comprehensive table is given in (ref. 28). The oceans contain 4 billion tons of natural uranium or about 3 milligrams per cubic meter. All the daughter products from the decay of uranium and thorium, including radium-226 and radon-222, are therefore found in sea water. Polonium-210 is an important alpha-emitter. Other important nuclides are potassium-40 and rubidium-87.

The ultimate fate of the released fission products will be a uniform global distribution in the oceans, a process that might take thousands of years. The fission products with short half-lives will decay during this process. The average concentration of the fission products of the reference submarine core – if they were all released, see Table 4 – will be 20 becquerels per cubic meter in a water column of 10^{17} cubic meters, which roughly corresponds to the North Atlantic Basin.

Explanatory frame: Properties of nuclear radiation

Alpha-particles are easily stopped in matter. In air the range is a few centimeters. They penetrate less than 1 millimeter in the skin. The danger is when materials emitting alpha-particles are inhaled (damage to the lungs) or if ingested (bone-seeking particles).

Beta-particles have a range in air between 10 centimeters and 20 meters depending on the energy they carry. They penetrate a thickness of 1–2 centimeters of water.

Gamma-rays are more difficult to stop depending on their energy. Their range in water could be about 1 meter, 15 centimeters in concrete or 6 cm in steel.

Living tissues are damaged by nuclear radiation. The damage is caused by the amount of energy absorbed by the tissue.

The increase in background radioactivity due to man-made radioactive elements

The natural background radioactivity in sea water gets an added component by transuranics and fission products from fall-out from nuclear weapons tests, the Chernobyl accident and from effluents from reprocessing plants. The transuranics plutonium-239 and plutonium-240 together with americium-241 have been observed in the North Sea and in UK coastal waters. They do not exist naturally and originate partly from fall-out from nuclear weapons tests and partly from effluents from nuclear reprocessing facilities. As a result of a survey which has been performed along the Norwegian coast from Hvaler to the Barents Sea, it was concluded that the transuranics observed there originate from fall-out from bomb tests only and not from the reprocessing plants in Europe (ref. 29). Concentration levels of 30–40 mBq/m^3 sea water have been measured off Greenland (ref. 30).

Explanatory frame: Units of nuclear radiation

The unit for measuring radioactivity is one becquerel (Bq) and is a measure of the number of disintegrations per second. In this book the tera becquerel (TBq) is a more practical unit, where 1 TBq = 10^{12} Bq. Radioactivity concentrations are given in becquerels per kilogram (Bq kg^{-1}). The old unit Curie (Ci) is defined as 3.7×10^{10} Bq.

The unit for absorbed dose is one gray (Gy). It is defined by the unit for energy, joule, per kilogram, $J\ kg^{-1}$. The radiation dose expresses how much energy has been absorbed by an organism, but tells nothing about the damage done. An absorbed dose of alpha-particles might represent a damage to tissue which is about 10 times higher than the same amount of energy from gamma-radiation. Alpha-radiation is given a 'quality factor' to make radiation damages comparable. If the unit for absorbed dose is multiplied by this quality factor, the unit 'dose equivalent' is established. It is called sievert (Sv) and means $J\ kg^{-1} \times$ (quality factor).

Dose-rate means energy absorbed per unit of time.

Fission products have been released into the Irish Sea from the reprocessing plant in Sellafield over a period of more than 35 years. The releases are well documented (refs. 31 and 33). They have been reduced substantially over the last 10 years due to the instalment of a new ion-exchange effluent and salt evaporator, fig. 36.

Fission products are also being released into the British Channel and the North Sea from the reprocessing plant in Cap de la Hague, close to Cherbourg in France.

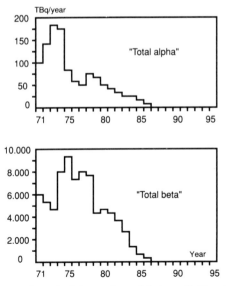

Fig. 38 Discharges of total alpha and total beta activities into the Irish Sea from Sellafield site during the years 1971 to 1987.

Elements of the dispersion problem

The surface water in the Norwegian, Greenland and Labrador Seas in the north and the Weddell Sea in the south is the principal source of the deep-sea water of the great oceans. The water sinks to the bottom because it is colder and has a higher salinity, and is therefore heavier. It is oxygen-rich as well. The bottom water flow in the North Atlantic has been measured recently (ref. 32) to be 10.7 million cubic-meters per second with an average velocity of 25–30 centimeters per second and a peak velocity of 100 cm/sec. This annual formation of deep and bottom water at high latitudes requires an upward return flow from the interior of the ocean. The spatial distribution of this return flow has not been established.

Geophysical processes of importance for deep-sea contaminant transport

The seabed water boundary layers range in thickness from a few meters over the abyssal plains to several tens of meters over high kinetic-energy zones along the continental rise and slope. They are formed by the friction arising from the flow of water against the bottom. The effects of fluctuations on the structure of the boundary level, and the dynamics and efficiency of mixing within them, are not yet sufficiently understood.

A dispersion scenario for describing the evolution of a release of fission products from its inception at a point source at the ocean bottom to its terminus at the ocean surface is given in (ref. 34). The principal physical processes thought to affect the transport and spreading of the material are presented in figs. 39 and 40.

Fig. 39 gives a visual impression of a number of physical processes that stir the bottom boundary level (BBL). BBL 'detachment' is a newly observed phenomenon which entails a dramatic ejection of fluid 'blobs' directly into the deep interior. These 'blobs' typically are about 10 km in size, but sometimes up to 100 km. Detachment events are thought to occur at intervals of about 100 days at some sites, but supporting data are sparse. Shear dispersion due to varying horizontal water velocities plays an important part in dispersing the material horizontally within the bottom boundary layer.

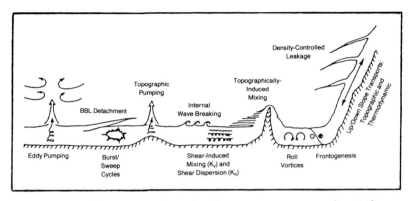

Fig. 39 Schematic representation of exchange processes occurring at the sea bottom and in the deep ocean (Robinson & Simmons).

Fig. 40 gives a visual description of how the dispersion could be defined in a number of stages, each stage dominated by different dispersion phenomena. A package of material quite limited in horizontal di-

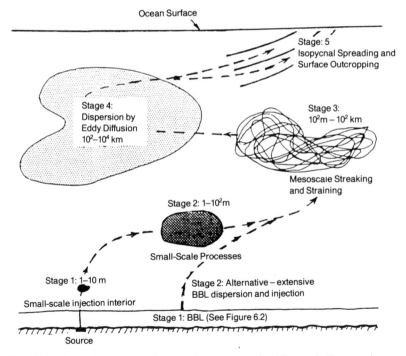

Fig. 40 A schematic presentation of release stages (Robinson & Simmons).

mensions (a few square meters) entering the deep interior could be spread by shear dispersion to about 100 square meters in a matter of days. Internal wave shearing and breaking add to this process.

Mixing and stirring are two complementary dispersion phenomena. Mixing is a homogenizing effect providing dispersion on the molecular level, whereas stirring involves distortion of a contaminant by a velocity shear field without significantly mixing the contaminant particles with the water molecules. Through this process it is possible for threads or patches of the origial contaminant cloud to be dispersed in such a way that each thread or patch contains a contaminant concentration that is high compared to the average in the overall region of dispersion. Due to this stirring, the concentration field of a contaminant released from a point source (submarine) will be streaky. Significant streakiness has been estimated to persist for periods of about one year and within a few hundred kilometers of the source.

The next stage is characterized by mesoscale eddy stirring and streaking, see fig. 40, (ref. 34). Once a material substance reaches a diameter of about 100 meters, mesoscale shearing may increase the size of the substance without diluting it. The domain becomes marbled with thin filaments of contaminated water. After a few months, the streaks have wrapped up to such an extent that they begin to overlap. After about a year, the domain reaches 100 kilometer in diameter and the stirring has marbled the contaminant throughout the eddy to the extent that small-scale diffusion smooths out the concentration to form a more uniform and cloud-like distribution. The time scale is months to years. The time scale for spreading to basin size is centuries, which is also the time required for vertical processes to have mixed the contaminant upward to a height of 3 000 meters above the bottom.

A general observation is that the large-scale circulation in the oceans is stably stratified. The water flow is along (imaginary) surfaces of the same density (isopycnals) and transport across these surfaces is small, but nevertheless important, compared to exchange along them. Once a material has reached a height 3 000 meters above sea bottom, it can come into contact with isopycnals that outcrop at the sea surface at higher latitudes. The mean thermohaline circulation along these isopycnals could lead to outcropping at the surface from mid-depths in time scales as small as 30 years.

The large-scale oceanographic processes are dominated by eddies and rings and extend over distances of several tens to hundreds of kilometers. Discrete eddies, called lenses, have been observed 10–100 kilometers in horizontal scale and have been detected thousands of kilometers from their source. It is not known how they are generated or how frequent they are. They can be transported relatively undiluted for thousands of kilometers before being absorbed into their surroundings. Their properties have been most closely documented for the upper 1–2 kilometers of the ocean, but they are known to occur at great depths.

It should be pointed out that the intensity of all these processes can vary considerably depending on the location. In the Gulf Stream area the mixing, eddying, shearing and deep and shallow mean flows are up to several hundred times more energetic than their mid-ocean counterparts, but in comparatively long, narrow zones.

An analogy: the smoke-filled room

A more popular description of what is meant by dispersion due to these physical processes can be provided by an analogy, the smoke-filled room (ref. 35).

Consider a closed room occupied by several people, one of whom is smoking. A plume of smoke is carried away by currents of air. The plume will twist and turn so that the concentration at any point in the vicinity of the smoker fluctuates considerably. At first only those people close to the smoker (the near-field) are affected.

However, the turbulent currents of air gradually carry and mix the smoke to the farthest extremities of the room (the far-field), and a general background level of smoke begins to build up. However, remnants of the concentrated plumes of smoke exist everywhere even though their concentration has been reduced by mixing. After a while the concentration of smoke will cease to increase so rapidly, as the processes of removing it from the air in the room, such as removal by ventilation and deposition on suitable surfaces (such as fabrics and lungs), begin to take effect.

Ultimately, if the smoker persists for long enough, a more or less steady state develops, with a background concentration field largely determined by the location and strength of the source and of the removal mechanisms, though somewhat distorted by whatever persistent currents of air which may exist in the room. The concentration of smoke is always highest close to the smoker, the near-field. Superimposed on this are various fluctuations, some due to the fluctuating position of the plume of smoke at any time, some due to unpredictable fluctuations of aircurrents bringing concentrations from elsewhere.

All these aspects mimic features of the expected behaviour of a radioactive contaminant in the ocean. Although the ocean is more complicated due to stratification, rotation, chemistry, biology etc., in a descriptive sense the processes of dispersion and the fluctuations and the steady state in the near-fields and far-fields remain the same. As pointed out in (ref. 34) it should be emphasized that although definite laws governing dispersion in the ocean have been put forward, they are preliminary, and there is no universally accepted quantitative theory to predict dispersion properly. However, the models developed have a basic message that time-scales for bottom to surface dispersion are roughly 200 to 2 000 years.

Geochemical and biological processes contribute to the dispersion

In addition to the physical dispersion processes described above, geo-chemical processes contribute considerably to the dispersion process. Most substances dissolved in sea water undergo a number of biochemical and/or geochemical interactions with the suspended particulate matter in ocean and marine sediments. Reactive substances are thus cycled between, on the one hand, the particulate material that primarily carries them to the deep ocean, and on the other hand, the water phase in which the reactive substances are carried away from the deep sea towards the ocean surface. This recycling may occur many times before the substance is either buried in the sediments or is removed by radioactive decay or degradation (ref. 34).

Suspended particulate matter (biomass, sediment particles etc.) binds water. The processes by which the reactive substances are removed from the dissolved water phase by particulate water is generally referred to as scavenging. There are three major steps in the scavenging process.

– The first is the biochemical and/or geochemical interactions leading to the contaminant associating with the particulate phase. Some sort of local equilibrium of the contaminant between dissolved and particulate phases will occur.

– The second is the transport of the contaminant in space while in the particulate phase. This transport will normally be very different from the transport in the dissolved phase, since sedimenting particles or faecal pellets or buoyant eggs (the particulates) tend to move down vertically across density surfaces.

– The third is the ultimate removal of the substances from the marine environment by processes such as incorporation in stable sedimentary formations.

The dispersion of radioactive material is influenced by biological processes as well. The total quantities of contaminants taken up by organisms – if accumulated and if the movements of biomass and organisms are sufficient – might be a significant part of the total mass transport, sufficient to alter the concentration field which would otherwise be established by physical and geochemical processes. Mass transport will take place only if the quantities of contaminant, biomass etc. involved are sufficiently large. Only gross quantities matter. On the other hand, a significant human exposure pathway may be created by a food chain which transports only a tiny fraction of the total quantity of contaminant, insufficient to have any discernible effect on the distribution.

Bioturbation is another biological dispersion process. This involves the movements of living species in the surface layers of the bottom sediments. Radioactive material has been observed to be transported downwards 10–20 centimeters by such processes.

The presence of a contaminant may affect the organisms themselves, and possibly cause damage to the ecosystem. This might occur in the regions where biological production is greatest, i.e. in the ocean surface layers and in the regions of shallow water. Such effects may be estimated once the concentration field and 'dose/effect' information is known, and may therefore be handled in a fashion similar to that used for food chains; indeed, food chains may be involved.

Dispersion modelling

The general problem confronting the public authorities once a nuclear submarine has come to rest on the seabed is threefold, first, to establish whether releases have taken place or not. Second, the problem is to predict where in the ocean the released material will go, when it will get there, how much will get there, and how confident one can be of the prediction. Thirdly, one needs to judge what damage, if any, can be expected to the marine species and/or to man.

Forecasts of where the released substances goes has to be based on physical models of the water movement. It is beyond the scope of this book to delve into the intricacies of the hydrodynamics of the oceans. Suffice to say that the models are based on well-known principles of conservation of water mass, momentum and energy. Once the water movement has been described, the effects on the dispersion of geochemical and biological processes can be superimposed.

The first task is to have the total model *verified*. This entails making sure that the physical, geochemical and biological processes involved are properly understood and applied, and that they are conveyed in a mathematical form which is adequate and without numerical flaws. Verification is therefore related to understanding the scientific and computational merits of the model.

The next step is to *validate* the model. Validating such a computer model involves demonstrating how closely the verified solutions of the mathematical model describe the real behaviour of the environment. Calculated distributions and concentrations of contaminants must be compared to distributions and concentrations which actually have been measured from specific known releases. In fact, 'radionuclide oceanography' is a growing discipline in oceanography, where the study of the behaviour and distributions of both natural and man-made radioisotopes is a new tool in the validation of oceanic circulation models.

The feasibility study of the disposal of high-level radioactive waste (ref. 34) made a considerable contribution to the development of a set of models which provide, within reasonable limits of expectations, such forecasts. Unfortunately, this study has been terminated at a point in time before models intended for the assessment of accidents during transport of highly radioactive waste canisters on the shelf or in shallow waters were developed. Such models would have been particularly relevant for the study of accidents involving nuclear submarines in shallow waters.

Adapting a dispersion model to a specific submarine site in the ocean is no easy task. There is no simple formula for doing this. A variety of models exist, one of which was developed for the dumping site for low-level radioactive waste in the North Atlantic. The purpose of the GESAMP studies was, in fact, to review present knowledge of the pathways by which substances might be transferred from a deep ocean dumping area to man. The recommendation (ref. 35) concludes that no single model is appropriate for all purposes.

Dispersion of fission products in the sea

There is no universal model for evaluating the short- and long-term effect of each of the existing six sunken submarines in the Atlantic. What information, then, is available to tell us something of the nature and magnitude of the risks which could apply to the next sunken submarine at location X?

Some known releases studied

Studies of the dispersion from known releases to the sea can be used for validation of dispersion models. Only one of these releases relates to deep sea dispersion. That is the dumping of low-level, long-lived radioactive waste from the civilian nuclear industry into specified dumping sites in the North Atlantic, see map fig. 41.

Other well known and controlled releases take place into shallow coastal areas and could be relevant for validation purposes:

- the release of low-level waste into the Irish Sea from the Sellafield site
- the release of low-level waste into the British Channel from the Cap de la Hague site in France
- the dispersion of 350 grams of plutonium in Arctic waters after an air crash at Thule, Greenland, involving nuclear weapons
- the dispersion into the Pacific of fission products and transuranics from the nuclear test fields at Bikini and Enewetak atolls

Study of these releases have contributed to the understanding of the mechanisms for the transport of fission products and transuranic materials in the waters and sediments.

Dispersion from nuclear waste dumps in the North Atlantic

The dumping of radioactive waste in the oceans is regulated by The Convention on the Prevention of Marine Dumping of Wastes and Other Matter which was approved and signed in London in 1972. The London Dumping Convention (LDC) resulted in the prohibition of dumping of high level radioactive waste in accordance with recommendations provided by The International Atomic Energy Agency (IAEA), the recognized expert body which offers scientific advice to the LDC on radioactive waste.

The IAEA has issued a document, "Definitions and Recommendations", in which permissible limits on radioactivity release rates from all sources are recommended. The document is revised regularly. In 1983 the parties to the LCD agreed on a moratorium suspending dumping of radioactive waste into the Atlantic for 10 years. Several countries voted against this moratorium, among them the United Kingdom, which reserves the right to dump large, low-level radioactive objects (like defuelled nuclear submarine reactor compartments) into the ocean.

The release rate limits of the 1979 review were based on a number of assumptions. The most important were:

- that the dumping site is located in an ocean about the size of the North Atlantic at depths more than 4 000 meters
- that the releases are going on *continuously* for a time corresponding to the mean life of Pu-239 (40 000 years)
- that the waste dumped was released immediately after reaching the seabed
- that 80 radionuclides are considered to be contributing to the world dose commitment through five individual pathways involving consumption of food
- that the release rate limits derived correspond directly, given the pathways and parameters used, to the ICRP dose limits for individual members of the public (refs. 36 and 37)

The dispersion model used was not site-specific. A generic model developed by the IAEA was applied. The reviewing panel considered it unlikely that doses to critical population groups in fact ever exceed or even equal 0.1 percent of relevant ICRP dose limits.

No release of radioactive material has been reported from the six sunken submarines in the Northern Atlantic. Radioactive waste has been dumped in the Atlantic at a number of sites shown on the map, fig. 41. The most important dumping site is some 700 kilometers northwest of Spain. The locations of the lost submarines are also shown. How do these two sources of leakage of radioactive substances to the environment compare?

Table 12 contains the (1979) recommended permissible release rates for the waste dumping site together with figures for the cumulative low-level radioactive waste actually dumped into the North Atlantic

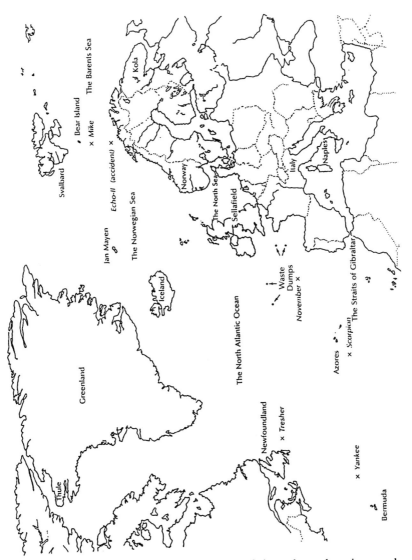

Fig. 41 Map of the Atlantic showing positions of six sunken submarines, and sites of dumping of radioactive waste.

between 1947 and 1982 and annual average dumping for the years 1978–1982 (ref. 38). The inventory of radioactive materials in a nuclear submarine is shown in the fourth column. These figures relate to the inventory after a lapse of 3 and 1000 days, respectively, after the submarine sinks. The radioactivity level of the British 'generic' reactor plant components is shown in the fifth column. It is calculated to be $3x10^3$ TBq one year after the shut-down of the reactor (ref. 39). The corresponding figure for the defuelled reactor compartment of the USS Sea Wolf plant, which was dumped into the Atlantic in 1960, is $1.2x10^3$ TBq.

	Release rate limit (TBq/y)	Dumped 1949–82	Ann.averages 1978–82 (TBq)	Inventory in reactor core (TBq)		Plant activity (TBq)
				3 days	1000 days	
Group A	$3.7x10^2$	0.23	–			
Group B	$3.7x10^3$	$6.8x10^2$	$0.7x10^2$	$1.4x10^2$	$1.4x10^2$	
Group C	$3.7x10^5$	$3.8x10^4$	$2.0x10^3$	$9.10x10^5$	$1.13x10^5$	$3x10^3$
Group D	$3.7x10^9$	$1.5x10^4$	$2.5x10^3$	$1.46x10^6$		

Group A: Ra-226 and very long-lived beta-gamma emitters
Group B: Most alpha emitters and transuranics (12 nuclear warheads)
Group C: Sr-90, Cs-137 and most beta-gamma emitters
Group D: Tritium and short-lived beta-gamma emitters

Table 12 Previously recommended release rate limits for dumping of radioactive waste in the Atlantic, amounts of waste dumped 1949–82, average annual dumping rate 1978–82, inventory in the reactor core, in the main components of the reactor primary system and in 12 (arbitrarily chosen) nuclear warheads (Group B).

Selective comparisons are daring, but in want of better data they have some interest. The total submarine inventory could have been released during one year without violating the limits set (now abandoned) for this dumping site. The inventory is higher than the actual amounts dumped. When setting the dumping limits the assumption was made that the waste dumped dissolves immediately after reaching the seabed, whereas the submarine will release at most a fraction of its radioactivity content. There is therefore a rationale for believing that a nuclear submarine resting on the seabed of the deep ocean will have a minor impact on the environment.

The suitability of the Atlantic dumping site was reviewed again in 1985 (ref. 38). A dispersion model specific to this dumping site was developed. Ocean circulation included the North and South Atlantic, the

Pacific, the Arctic, the Antarctic and the Indian Ocean. Collective doses and the effects on marine organisms were considered. In order to give an indication of the doses to individuals (critical groups) that did or would arise, three scenarios were considered. These were related to the effects of:

a. past dumping rates
b. past dumping plus a further five years of dumping at rates typical of recent years in which dumping took place, and
c. past dumping plus five years dumping at ten times that rate

The conclusion was that for all three scenarios, the doses to members of the critical groups were less than 2×10^{-7} Sv per year, i.e. less than 0.02 percent of the 1 mSv per year level suggested by ICRP as a maximum for exposures over long periods.

The dispersion model used was later criticised in the Feasibility Study referred to earlier (ref. 34) by pointing to the fact that simple dispersion models that include some physics, some geo-chemistry and some biology might be easily solvable but will provide results of dubious reliability.

Release of long-lived radioactive waste from the Sellafield reprocessing facility into the Irish Sea

Releases of radioactive waste into the Irish Sea are well documented and have taken place for more than 30 years (ref. 33). The distribution of the radioactive nuclides in the water column and in the sediments on the bottom of the sea and the up-take of radioactive products in fish, shellfish and other organisms have been measured. The data will be invaluable in any validation scheme for dispersion models.

The releases into the Irish Sea of the most important long-lived nuclides are well documented (ref. 33). The effluents discharged do not contain short-lived nuclides. The caesium-137 concentrations have been measured at various locations in the Irish Sea, see figs. 42 and 43. It can be clearly seen that the concentrations decrease with increasing distance from the source. Fig. 38 shows the total amount of beta and gamma activities discharged into the Irish Sea over the last 15 years (ref. 31).

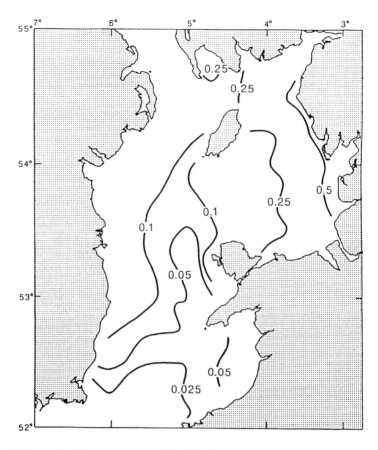

Fig. 42 Caesium-137 concentration (Bq/kg) distribution in the Irish Sea, April 1987.

The nuclides which are easily carried with sea water (like caesium-137) are flushed from the Irish Sea into Scottish waters and further into the North and the Norwegian Seas. The estimated transit time between the Sellafield site and the North Channel of the Irish Sea is estimated to be one year or less (ref. 33). Transport around northern Scotland to the southern North Sea, see figs. 42, 43 and 44, is estimated to take about 3 years. Some 10 percent of the total caesium-137 discharges is contained in sediments in the northern part of the Irish Sea. More than 90 percent of the total discharge of caesium-137 will eventually reach the Norwegian Sea. This also applies to strontium-90, tritium and technetium-99.

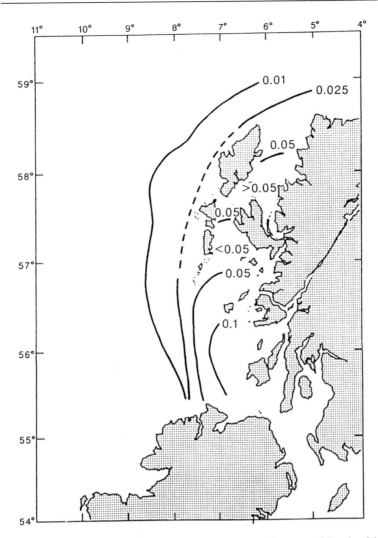

Fig. 43 Concentration (Bq/kg) of caesium-137 from the west of Scotland into the North Sea, April 1987.

The main circulation around the British Isles, the North Sea and the west European continental shelf waters has been thoroughly investigated. Several numerical models have been developed and validated using radioactive tracers from Sellafield and Cap de la Hague. Prandle (ref. 40) has calculated the 'age' distribution (in years) for the effluents

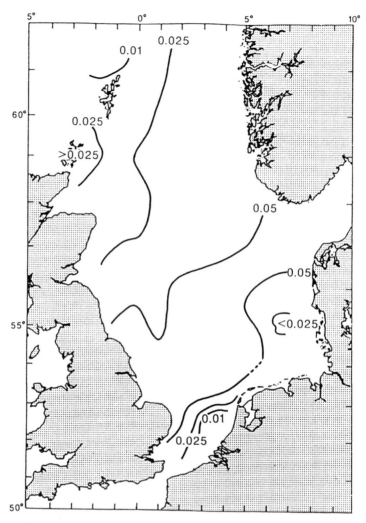

Fig. 44 Distribution of caesium-137 in the North Sea due to releases from Sellafield and Cap de la Hague reprocessing facilities, August-September 1987.

of Sellafield and Cap de la Hague. The 'age' of a constituent of a water-mass is defined as the average time it needs to travel from its discharge position to another arbitrary position in the area under consideration, see fig. 45.

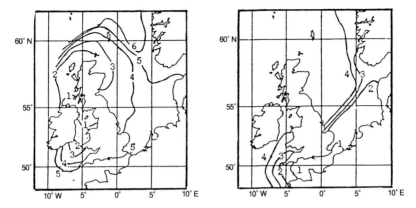

Fig. 45 Average time (years) needed for caesium-137 to travel from Sellafield (left) and Cap de la Hague (right) to another arbitrary position.

Dahlgaard et al. (ref. 41) have reported that the Sellafield effluent reaches the East Greenland current in about 6–8 years. If say, the concentration is set at 1 000 in the northern Irish Sea where the material stays for 1 year it will take about 3 years to cross the North Sea, during which time its concentration drops to 100. The passage along the Norwegian Coast takes another year, with a dilution of another 50 percent, and by the time the material reaches the waters near Greenland, within 2–4 years, its concentration will be about one thousandth of its original value.

Dispersion of plutonium and transuranics in the sea and sediments

The total plutonium inventory of a sunken submarine, whether nuclear or not, might give rise to a serious contamination problem. The very low solubility of plutonium in sea water, however, ensures that the problem is not an acute one.

The dispersion mechanisms

The plutonium embedded in the reactor fuel elements, if any, is reasonably well protected. The dissolution rate is expected to be low, although no numerical evidence for this can be offered.

The plutonium in nuclear warheads is more vulnerable. The barriers protecting the environment will be the warhead capsule only, although the hull might give some resistance to free water circulation. Scenarios for what might happen to that plutonium could be:

– the nuclear warheads are fully intact after sinking
– the nuclear warheads implode in one way or another during sinking and lumps of plutonium are spread inside the submarine or on the seabed
– the nuclear warheads are (according to instructions?) destroyed by chemical explosives to avoid being captured. The plutonium will be partly pulverized and spread over a limited area

In the case of intact warheads in shallow waters, the problem is primarily one of a salvage operation. It will probably take years before the protective barriers surrounding the explosives deteriorate due to corrosion. A salvage operation is therefore, technically speaking, not urgent. Political pressures might, however, favour fast salvaging.

The extent to which the plutonium will pulverize during a destruction phase is uncertain. Lumps of plutonium metal will oxidise in the sea water via a hydroxide phase. Plutonium oxide has a low solubility in sea water. Less than 1 percent per year will dissolve and start dispersing through the water volume. About that much will also dissolve, but this part will adhere to particles in the water and sink to the bottom not far from the source point.

The sea bottom currents will float bottom sediment particles which will settle farther away and thereby move the plutonium. The important effect tending to temporarily immobilize the plutonium is that it penetrates into the bottom sediments. This process turns out to be quite fast. Plutonium seems to be strongly attached to the sediments. Clay is an efficient adsorber of plutonium oxide. However, re-suspension into the water column has been observed.

The Thule nuclear weapon accident

In January 1968 a US B-52 bomber carrying four nuclear weapons crashed 11 kilometers east of Thule in Greenland. The warheads were equipped with the non-sensitive chemical explosive, see chapter 4. No nuclear explosions occurred, but the warheads burned and their contents of plutonium, americium, uranium and tritium were spread over a limited area. The total release amounted to 3 150 grams of which 350 grams were trapped in the ice. The rest was recovered and removed. Sedimentation studies of melted ice cores showed that 85 to 95 percent of the debris and associated plutonium oxide sank when the ice broke up in June-July 1968.

The spread of plutonium on the seabed in this area has been thoroughly investigated and documented by A. Aarkrog, (refs. 42 and 43). That same year a plutonium contamination was found within a distance of 15 kilometers from the source point. In 1970 this distance had increased to 30 kilometers, and by 1974 to 45 kilometers. The median distance seems to have increased by 0.4 kilometers per year for the period 1974–1979.

Two years after the crash-landing, the plutonium oxide had penetrated at least 10 cm down into the bottom sediment. The spread was caused partly by bottom currents which float contaminated bottom sediments and partly by the bioturbulent activity in the sediments which transport the plutonium downwards. Plutonium has been observed in the benthic fauna, in shellfish, fish and shrimps, but only in very small amounts. The transfer decreases for each level in the nutrition chain. It has been concluded (ref. 43) that the contamination after the Thule accident has not created health problems for humans and there are no indications of bioamplification of plutonium and americium through the marine nutrition chain in the Thule area. It should be pointed out, however, that all data from the Thule accident is site-specific and therefore only of limited value for comparison purposes. The results could be quite different with a different marine flora and fauna.

The spread of plutonium from the weapons test areas on the Bikini and Enewetak atolls

The nuclear weapons tests on the Bikini and Enewetak Atolls ended in 1958. The sediments in these atolls contain plutonium and americium in addition to large amounts of fission products. The transuranics are unevenly distributed, but can be observed down to 16 cm in the sediments (ref. 44). The amount of plutonium at Enewetak have been estimated by Noshkin and Wong (ref. 44) to be about 250 Curies (9.3 TBq) in the first 2.5 cm of the sediments, and the amount down to 16 cm is about 1 200 Ci (44.4 TBq). At the Bikinis the corresponding numbers are 309 Ci (11.4 TBq) and 1 470 Ci (54.4 TBq).

It has been observed that the content of Pu in the sea water in and around the atolls is considerably higher than that measured elsewhere as a result of the fall-out from the weapons test program. This plutonium must therefore originate from the sediments through dissolution. The concentration of Pu in sea water in the lagoons has been relatively constant over a reported period from 1965 to 1978. The water volumes are replenished continuously by new sea water containing only background levels of transuranics. The plutonium washed out is then dispersed in the sea outside the atolls.

The observed inventories in the lagoon waters are 0.9 Ci (0.033 TBq) at Enewetak and 1.3 Ci (0.048 TBq) at the Bikinis. Of these, 44 percent will be attached to particles in the water volumes and will sink to the bottom again, whereas the rest will be in chemical solution and be transported out of the lagoon.

At Enewetak the amount in solution represents 0.36 percent of the amount, 250 Ci (9.3 TBq) fixed to the upper 2.5 cm of the sediments, and 0.075 percent of the total amount, 1 200 Ci (44.4 TBq) down to 16 cm. This reflects the slower circulation from the test water column to the water column above. At Bikini the corresponding figures are 0.40 percent of 309 Ci (11.4 TBq) and 0.086 percent of 1 470 Ci (54.4 TBq).

Estimates of water circulation through the lagoons have been given: at Enewetak the average residence time of the water is estimated to be 144 days. Accordingly, 2.8 Ci(0.1 TBq) will be transported from the lagoon annually, which amounts to 0.2 percent of the total or 1 percent of the amount in the upper 2.5 cm.

If the inventory down to 16 cm in the sediment column (1 200 curies) is the reservoir for the mobilized plutonium at Enewetak, then the mean life for the plutonium in this reservoir is about 430 years. The corresponding mean life for the plutonium at Bikini is 460 years (ref. 44).

Release of transuranics to the Irish Sea from the reprocessing plant in Sellafield

Another piece of information of value for validation of dispersion models is the release of transuranics to the Irish Sea from the reprocessing plant in Sellafield. Between 1960 and 1981 660 TBq of plutonium, corresponding to about 300 kg, together with 520 TBq of americium were released into the Irish Sea (ref. 38). The British Directorate of Fisheries Research has studied the distribution of transuranics in the Irish Sea. A continued reduction of the release is expected with the instalment of the Enhanced Actinide Removal Plant scheduled for 1992.

Plutonium and americium have been observed in sea water, fish and shellfish and in marine plants. Studies have shown that the plutonium is adsorbed to particles in the sea water and sinks to the bottom fast. More than 90 percent of the plutonium is adsorbed to the sediments. The remainder stays afloat in the water column, finely distributed, over extended areas in the Irish Sea. A small fraction behaves like caesium-139 and is transported from the Irish Sea to the Atlantic and North and Norwegian Seas. Enhanced levels of plutonium-239/240, compared with fall-out levels from nuclear weapons tests, have been detected in the North Sea.

Particles that settle on the bottom are sedimented over time. Bore tests have been made and the distribution of transuranics has been measured down to depths of 25–30 cm. To which extent the plutonium adsorbed to the sediments can be released again is a subject for study. A certain resuspension of the surface layers has been observed.

The bulk of the transuranics will be bound to the sediments, but a lesser part will be absorbed by marine plants, fish and shellfish. The use of a special weed, porphyra, in a regional laverbread which was consumed by a local inhabitants, made it necessary some time ago to define this group as a 'critical population group'. In order to keep radiation dosages to this group below internationally accepted limits, it was nessessary to set upper limits to acceptable releases. This weed is no longer harvested in the Irish Sea (but not because of releases from Sellafield).

Another comparison can put the contamination problem in a certain perspective: the natural isotope polonium-210 which is absorbed in fish flesh gives a radiation dose through consumption of the fresh fish. Polonium-210 has a half-life of 138.4 days and emits alpha particles like plutonium. It gives, according to Pentreath et al. (ref. 45), a contribution to the radiation dose for the population which is 1 percent of ICRP's permissible upper limits. This is 100 times higher than the contributions from the transuranics plutonium-americium in the same fish.

Dispersion of the submarine plutonium inventory

The total amount of submarine plutonium (including 12 nuclear warheads) can be compared with the annual permissible release rate from the dumping site in the North Atlantic for radioactive waste from the civilian nuclear power industry. A moratorium on this dumping is now in force. This comparison is shown in Table 4. The inventory could, as shown, safely have been released at this dumping site within a year without violating the limits established at that time. This comparison is not valid for the actual locations of the six sunken submarines without further substantiation.

No attempts have been made to analyze the dispersion to the environment from any of the locations of the sunken submarines. The experiences from Bikini, Enewetak and Thule indicate that dispersion will take place slowly and that its progress will be site-specific and dependent on the initial spread of the plutonium.

The dispersion issue, however, is only part of the overall problem. The health hazard of performing a salvage operation will very much depend on the plutonium contamination of the submarine wreck. Before any salvage operation can be undertaken, the extent of contamination must be investigated. There is a special problem with salvaging Soviet submarines with bismuth-lead liquid-metal cooled propulsion plants. Neutrons absorbed in the bismuth during operation create the isotope polonium-210. As mentioned earlier, this isotope has a half-life of 138.4 days and is an alpha emitter. This is a very unpleasant form of radioactivity and can constitute a contamination problem for the salvaging operation, if the coolant is exposed to sea water. However, the problem diminishes with time. Four years after the accident the radioactivity of the polonium-210 isotope is reduced to one tenth of one percent of the original value.

Dose rates to marine species and the pathway to man

If a nuclear submarine should sink in shallow waters and substantial proportions of its fission product inventory are released to the sea, what impact could this have on marine species and on man? No evaluations exist on this question. Neither does this book provide an answer, but the question must be asked anyway. Some light will hopefully be shed on the subject by referring to 'another street-light where the light is better'!

Impact on marine species

For illustration purposes, it can be mentioned that observed levels of radioactive products in fish and shellfish around the British Isles are on the order of 40–100 Bq/kg, and in seaweed 200–600 Bq/kg. This is mostly potassium-40 but includes caesium-137 and caesium-134.

The uptake of non-natural radioactive substances in marine species is a dynamic process. The uptake proceeds until an equilibrium has been established. In fish this might take weeks to months, see fig. 46.

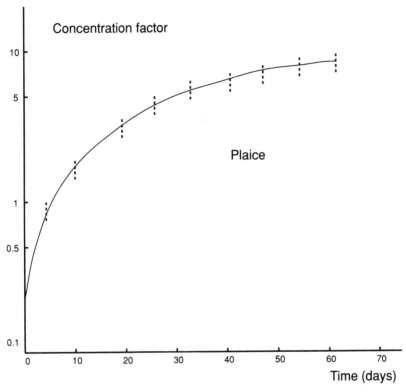

Fig. 46 The time dependence of experimental uptake of radioactive material in plaice under laboratory conditions.

Concentration levels (defined as quantity per unit weight of material divided by quantity of activity per unit volume of water) at equilibrium are taken from Clark and Webb (ref. 45) and shown for easy reference in Table 13 for some selected radioisotopes and marine species.

| Marine concentration factors (Bq/kg per Bq/liter) | | | | |
Radionuclide	Fish	Crustacean	Molluscs	Sediments
H-3	1	1	1	0
C-14	$5x10^3$	$5x10^3$	$5x10^3$	$1x10^2$
Co-58	$1x10^2$	$1x10^3$	$1x10^3$	$1x10^4$
Sr-90	1	$1x10^1$	$1x10^1$	$5x10^2$
Fe	$1x10^3$	$1x10^3$	$1x10^3$	$1x10^4$
Ni	$5x10^2$	$1x10^2$	$1x10^2$	$1x10^4$
Tc-99	$1x10^1$	$1x10^3$	$1x10^3$	$1x10^4$
Ru-106	1	$5x10^2$	$2x10^3$	$1x10^4$
I-129	$1x10^1$	$1x10^2$	$1x10^2$	$1x10^2$
Cs-134	$5x10^1$	$3x10^1$	$3x10^1$	$5x10^2$
Pu-239	$1x10^1$	$1x10^2$	$1x10^3$	$5x10^4$

Table 13 Concentration factors of some radionuclides in seafood and sediments.

The marine concentration factor is an important parameter in any assessment of the damage suffered by marine species from radioactive pollution.

The damage to marine species is determined by dose rate and exposure time. The dose rate depends on the radioactivity concentrations in sea water and on the dynamics of uptake concentrations in marine species for each individual nuclide and species.

Due to the complexity of the biological damage processes the calculation of dose rate is not a straightforward procedure and would require work beyond the scope of the present study. However, a survey of natural and man-made exposures of marine species taken from an IAEA Panel Summary Report (27) is shown for illustrative purposes in fig. 47. Ranges are given for exposures due to natural radioactivity in the marine environment, fall-out from nuclear weapons tests, releases into the Irish Sea and from other sources.

Ranges of exposure are also given for a number of biological experiments. Dose rates due to releases from a sunken submarine will be too site- and release-rate specific to make a meaningful comparison.

Fig. 47 (p. 155) Survey of natural and man-made exposures of marine species. Ranges of environmental dose rate experienced by fish (·—·) and ranges of dose rate employed in laboratory experiments with fish eggs and fish (×—×). In these experiments effects were *not* always apparent at the low end of the range.

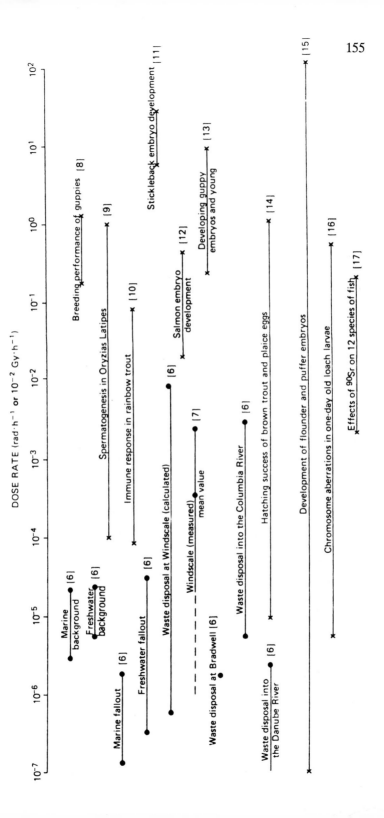

DOSE RATE (rad·h⁻¹ or 10⁻² Gy·h⁻¹)

Marine background [6]

Freshwater background [6]

Freshwater fallout [6]

Marine fallout [6]

Waste disposal at Windscale (calculated) [6]

Windscale (measured) mean value [7]

Waste disposal at Bradwell [6]

Waste disposal into the Columbia River [6]

Waste disposal into the Danube River [6]

Breeding performance of guppies [8]

Spermatogenesis in Oryzias Latipes [9]

Immune response in rainbow trout [10]

Stickleback embryo development [11]

Salmon embryo development [12]

Developing guppy embryos and young [13]

Hatching success of brown trout and plaice eggs [14]

Development of flounder and puffer embryos [15]

Chromosome aberrations in one-day old loach larvae [16]

Effects of ⁹⁰Sr on 12 species of fish [17]

There are two ways in which the results of dosimetric calculations can be examined: one is to compare the values with those estimated to pertain to the natural background, and the other is to compare the values with those which are known to result in harmful effects on marine organisms. Such comparisons can be made from fig. 47.

The pathway to man

The pathway to man of releases of radioactive material from sunken submarines can be rather long and difficult to assess. However, the contribution to collective dose commitments for the British population from the release of fission products into the Irish Sea has been assessed.

The Irish Sea is a rich fishing area. There are no areas where fishing is prohibited, even close to the point of release. Transuranics have been found in the fish flesh, in the large intestine tract and in the skeleton. The radioactivity level in the large intestine tract in plaice, which is a bottom fish, is particularly pronounced.

The radiation dose to consumers from fish and shellfish depends upon both the amount consumed and the radioactivity concentration. A wide range in annual doses between individuals is to be expected. Potential exposures to the British population have been estimated based on the consumption of fish and shellfish from the Irish Sea. The 'critical group' approach has been used, which is based upon identifying groups of individuals from populations subject to the highest radiation exposures. The radiation concentrations are highest in the vicinity of the effluent pipeline. Hence, consumers within the local community are an exposed population whose consumption rate has been studied and kept under review.

Consumption rate surveys have shown that other population groups contain consumers of large quantities of fish and shellfish. These groups are also being reviewed, but their supplies come from fishing grounds farther away from the pipeline and accordingly the radioactivity concentrations are lower.

For the most heavily exposed critical group in the local fishing community close to the Sellafield site, individual radiation exposures in 1986 due to consumption of fish and shellfish from the Irish Sea have been estimated by Hunt (ref. 33) and are shown in Table 14. The consumption rate is shown in kg/year together with the contribution of relevant nuclides to the 'committed effective dose equivalent' in units of milli-Sieverts per year (mSv/year).

	Consumption rate		Nuclide	Committed eff. dose equiv. mSv/year
	kg/year	(grams/day)		
Fish:	36.5	(100)	Sr-90	0.006
Crustaceans	6.6	(18)	Ru-106	0.009
Molluscs	6.6	(18)	Cs-134	0.002
			Cs-137	0.038
			Pu-238	0.017
			Pu-239 + Pu-240	0.080
			Pu-241	0.036
			Am-241	0.150
			Total	0.34

Table 14 Individual radiation exposure of a specific critical population group due to consumption of Irish Sea fish and shellfish, 1986.

As can be seen from Table 14, the largest contribution comes from the transuranics (Pu-238, 239, 240, 241 and Am-241) which have detrimental effects on different cells in the body. They are much less mobile than most of the fission products and therefore have relatively high local concentrations.

Individual radiation exposure has decreased considerably over the last 10 years. The development over time is shown in fig. 48.

It should be stressed that the average exposure of the British population from the consumption of fish and shellfish from the Irish Sea is much less than this. The exposure of the 'critical group' in 1986 should be compared with the recommended ICRP dose limit of 1 mSv/year. For the previous years, fig. 48, these values are in excess of 1 mSv/year but within the ICRP subsidiary dose limit of 5 mSv which applies to members of the public.

The exposure of the British population from natural radioactivity is of the order of 2.2 mSv/year.

Total releases from 1957 to 1981 into the Irish Sea of the fission products which have long half-lives, caesium-139, caesium-134 and strontium-90 (ref. 38) are shown in fig. 49 together with corresponding inventories in a 100-megawatt propulsion plant. The inventories are given for 3 and 1000 days' decay after a potential accident. The inventories are (except for Cs-134) of the same order of magnitude as the total releases.

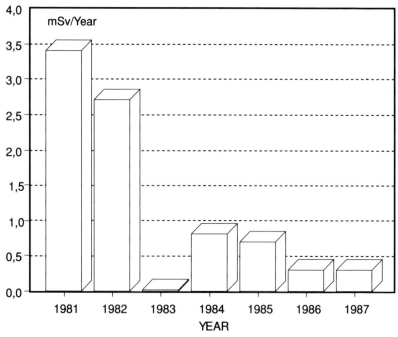

Fig. 48 Individual total radiation exposure of a particular critical group due to consumption of fish and shellfish from the Irish Sea, 1981–1988.

The total submarine inventory, see Table 9, is much larger: about 2200 'thousand tera-becquerels', to quote the units used. As an illustration (not an assessment!), 10 percent of the submarine inventory could be released over a period of 40 years without exceeding an annual release rate from Sellafield of 6 'thousand tera-becquerels' of 'total beta' as shown in fig. 34. A mere comparison of numbers of tera-becquerels, on the other hand, is a rather primitive exercise. Those who are better informed should make their knowledge available.

An assessment of the risk and the potential consequences of a nuclear submarine accident in the Irish Sea is beyond the scope of this book. In fact, if an accident should happen, the outcome could range from no release at all to something like the illustration above. In the case of no release, the mandatory salvaging operation will be a relatively easy task. In other cases, whose backyard will be open?

☆☆☆

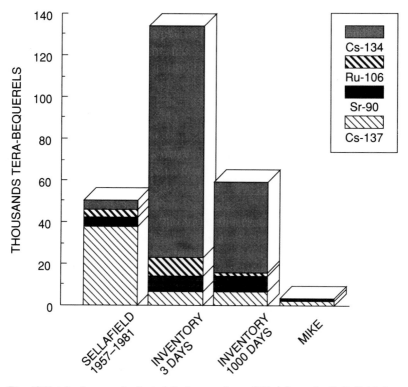

Fig. 49 Total releases of selected fission products (TBq) from the Sellafield site into the Irish Sea during 1957–1981, and inventories of the same fission products in a submarine at 3 and 1 000 days after an accident. The corresponding values from the sunken Soviet submarine Mike are also shown.

Epilogue

The magnitude of the consequences of an accident with a nuclear submarine is of course a trivial problem compared to the overall risks of a nuclear war. However, the risks are additive and can be reduced independently. The present international political climate has already led to a substantial reduction in the number of nuclear weapons. Intermediate-range nuclear missiles are being destroyed. Under the umbrella of the START negotiations a Treaty agreeing on a 30 percent reduction of landbased intercontinental ballistic missiles has been signed, and negotiations on further reductions have started. A complete abolition of all tactical nuclear weapons is a distinct possibility. A substantial reduction of the intercontinental nuclear missiles and instalment of most of the remaining missiles in submarines could be an overall positive development, but at the expense of increased safety risks.

A comprehensive environmental assessment should be undertaken by the appropriate authorities as a part of a plan for better preparedsness for the next accident. It would help matters considerably if it could be demonstrated under which conditions environmental damage from sunken submarines can or cannot be tolerated. In fact, an environmental assessment may not only provide better preparedness, it could also indicate some means of prevention, and it could imply, with a change of scope, a continuation of the international collaboration on The Feasibility of Disposal of High-level Radioactive Waste into the Seabed (ref. 34). This work has most unfortunately been terminated. Surveillance of all the existing sunken submarines should be entrusted to the International Atomic Energy Agency in Vienna.

Under the auspices of the International Maritime Organization, IMO, a Code of Safety for the design of *civilian* nuclear-propelled ships has been drawn up. The Soviet Union makes reference to this Code when describing their nuclear cargo-ship. Corresponding national codes of safety for naval nuclear ships must be presumed to exist. The navies will most probably refuse to relax their stringent secrecy concerning the design of the nuclear propulsion plants on the grounds that any released information will put at risk national security. Most design features have to be kept secret. On the other hand, it is hard to see how a candid public appraisal of a propulsion plant's safety barriers (possibly with the exception of the fuel cladding) could reveal secrets about the submarine's combat power, at least when it comes to evaluating whether and how a submarine could be a source of contamination on the seabed.

To sum up, how serious really is the threat of a sunken nuclear submarine to the environment? It is hard to establish a qualified opinion. There is not sufficient information in the public domain to do so. The range of potential risks is very wide. My book raises more questions than it answers. Firstly, one whould keep in mind that a nuclear propulsion plant is relatively small compared to a civilian nuclear power station. There has to be more than 30 units of the reference plant (100 MW) referred to in this book or 65 Rubis plants to make up for one Chernobyl power plant. Secondly, it is crucial to a judgement how and where the submarine is resting: either in a sealed low-risk condition on the bottom of the deep oceans or in a high-risk condition in a shallow coastal region with a damaged, leaky nuclear plant. Thirdly, no assessment has been made of the impact of the several hundred kilograms of plutonium contained in a SSBN with, say, 24 MIRVed missiles.

So whom should we believe? On the one hand the navies tell us there is nothing to worry about. As far as they go, they are right. In the present sunken submarines the reactors are sealed and there are no leakages. But there is obviously more to it than that.

At the other end of the scale we have the environmentalists rightly worried about the threats to a sacred environment. Let us by all means listen to them, since they have a valid point. Then there are the mass media which will drum up doomsday prophesies of potential damages for lack of facts. However, a sunken nuclear submarine is not the end of the world.

There is one side of the problem which warrents considerable caution. Some countries are extremely vulnerable to unjustified claims of radioactive pollution of marine food. Iceland earns 80 percent of its national income from the fishing industry! The mass media, through, have a duty to inform the public if, where and when actual releases have occurred. Knowledge and an extreme openness and candour about safety matters are a prerequisite for a balanced presentation of the true risks.

From my vantage point (under the nearest 'street-light'), all matters regarding nuclear submarines are cloaked in darkness. My hope is that the problems I have described in this book bear an acceptable relation to the international security which we stand to gain; but my fear is that they could simply be tips of an iceberg. So who can tell you the truth? Let the navies tell you!

Appendices

Vessel type	Submarines			Air.carr.	Cruisers	Ice-br.	Sum
	SSBN	SSGN	SSN				
United States	43(2)	–	114(10)	5(2)	9(–)	–	191(14)
Soviet Union	65+14	50(1)	85(15)	0(2)	2(2)	5(1)	221(21)
United Kingdom	6(2)	–	17(1)	–	–	–	23(3)
France	6(2)	–	6(2)	1(1)	–	–	13(5)
	134(6)	50(1)	222(28)	6(5)	11(2)	5(1)	428(43)

Table 1 Survey of nuclear propelled ships deployed or on order ( ) in 1989. Western submarines carrying cruise missiles are counted as attack submarines (SSN).

Fission prod.	Halflife	Activity buildup (10⁵TBq) 100 MW 600 days	Activity decay (10⁵TBq)			Waste category
			3 days	100 days	1000 days	
1 Noble gases						
Krypton-85	10.6y	0.096	0.096	0.094	0.080	
Xenon-133	5.28d	2.07	–	–	–	
2 Halogens						
Iodine-131	8.05d	0.97	0.75	nil	–	D
Iodine-132	0.1d	1.50	0.79			D
Iodine-133	21h	2.16	0.20			D
Iodine-135	6.7h	1.91	–	–	–	D
3 Alkali metals						
Caesium-134	2.05y	1.11	1.11	1.01	0.44	C
Caesium-136	13d	0.002	0.0017			
Caesium-137	30y	0.0724	0.0724	0.072	0.068	C
4 Chalogens						
Antimon-125	2.4y	0.0025	0.0025	0.0023	0.002	
Tellur-125m	57.4	0.00075	0.00075	0.00069	0.0006	
Antimon-127	3.88d	0.0817	0.0488			
Tellur-127	9.35h	0.0107	0.0107	0.0055		
Tellur-127m	105d	0.0107	0.0107	0.0055		
Tellur-129	74m	0.111	0.105	0.0137		
Tellur-129m	33d	0.111	0.105	0.0137		
Tellur-131m	30h	0.138	–	–		
Tellur-132	3.25d	1.502	0.792			
5 Strontium-89	51d	1.50	1.50	0.386	–	D
Strontium-90	28y	0.0724	0.0724	0.0719	0.067	C
Barium-137m	0.0018d	0.067	0.067	0.066	0.062	C
Barium-140	12.8d	2.0	2.0	0.0088		D

6 Metals

Nuclide	Half-life					Group
Molybdenum-99	2.8d	1.90	0.904	—	—	C
Ruthenium-103	41d	0.94	0.89	0.173	—	C
Rhodium-103m	0.039d	0.94	0.89	0.173	—	D
Ruthenium-106	366d	0.081	0.081	0.067	0.012	D
Rhodium-106	3.5×10^{-4}d	0.081	0.081	0.067	0.012	C

7 Lanthanides

Nuclide	Half-life					Group
Yttrium-90	2.68d	0.072	0.072	0.072	0.067	C
Yttrium-91	58d	1.69	1.69	0.51	—	D
Zirconium-95	63.2d	1.94	1.88	0.65	—	D
Niobium-95	35d	1.94	1.88	0.65	—	D
Niobium-95m	84h	0.0485	0.047	0.016	—	D
Zirconium-97	17h	1.85	0.10	—	—	D
Lanthan-140	40h	2.0	2.0	0.0088	—	D
Cerium-141	32.3d	1.88	1.76	0.22	—	
Cerium-143	33h	1.78	0.39	—	—	
Cerium-144	284d	1.44	1.41	1.13	0.126	C
Praseodym-144	0.012d	1.44	1.41	1.13	0.126	C
Praseodym-143	13.7d	1.90	1.75	0.13	—	C
Neodym-147	11.1d	0.78	0.66	0.002	—	
Prometium-147	2.6y	0.30	0.30	0.28	0.145	C
Sum Group B			9.10	4.53		
Sum Group C		10.4	14.6	2.45	1.13	
Sum Group D		21.4			—	

Group A: Ra-226 and very long-lived beta-gamma emitters
Group B: Most alpha emitters and transuranics
Group C: Sr-90, Cs-137 and most beta-gamma emitters
Group D: Tritium and short-lived beta-gamma emitters

Table 4 Uranium-235 fission product inventory in one 100 MW nuclear plant operated at full power for 600 days. Inventories are given for decay times after shut down of reactor of 3, 100 and 1000 days. Fission products with half-lives of just hours or less have been eliminated. Waste categories C and D are given as outlined in IAEA-211. All fissions are assumed to be due to fissions of uranium-235 only. Group B, the transuranics, are not present in a highly enriched fuel.

Radio-nuclide	Halflife	Bq/m³	Radio-nuclide	Halflife	Bq/m³
Potassium-40	1.25x10⁹y	1.1x10⁴	Thorium-234	24.1 d	37
Rubidium-87	4.7x10¹⁰y	1.1x10³	Protactinium-234	1.14 min	3.7x10³
Iodine-129	1.7x10⁷y	1.0	Uranium-234	2.48x10⁵y	38-48
Lead-210	19.4 y	3.3	Uranium-235	7.1x10⁸y	1.5-2.8
Polonium-210	138.4 d	3.3	Uranium-238	4.5x10⁹y	33-42
Polonium-218	3.05 min	3.3	Tritium-3	12.26y	6.0
Radon-222	3.8d	3.3	Beryllium-7	53d	<630
Radium-226	1 622y	3.3	Carbon-14	5 570y	3-5

Table 11 Concentrations of some natural radionuclides in the sea

Country Sub. type	Constr. time	Units	Displ. dived tons	Diving depths (m) Norm.	Max	Speed (kn) Surf.	div.	React. type	Power SHP	Mwatt	Refueling time (y)
USA											
SSBN											
Ohio	1979–	14(2)	18 700	300	–	20+		S8G	60 000	220	9
Lafayette	1963-67	29	8 250			18	25	S5W	15 000	70	6
SSN											
Los Angeles	1974–	56(10)	6 927	450			31	S6G	35 000	130	
Glenard P. Lipscong	1971	1	6 480				25+	S5Wa	15 000	70	
Narwhal	1966	1	5 350			20+	30+	S5G	17 000	70	
Sturgeon	1967-75	37	4 640	400		20+	30+	S5W	15 000	70	
Ethan Allen	1959-62	2	7 880			20+	30+	S5W	15 000	70	

Class	Years	No.	Displacement	Depth		Speed		Reactor	Power	
Permit	1959–67	13	4 300			20+	30+	S5W	15 000	70
Tullibee	1958	1	2 640			15+	20+	S2C	2 500	20
Skipjack	1956–61	3	3 513			16+	30+	S5W	15 000	70
Seawolf	1996–		9 150				34/35	S6W	60 000	220 / 15+
Soviet Union										
SSBN										
Typhoon	1981–	6	25 000				30+	2xPWR	100 000	330–360
Delta-IV	1984–	6	13 550				24	2xPWR	60 000	2x120
Delta-III	1974–82	14	13 250			18	24	2xPWR	50 000	
Delta-II	1974–75	4	12 750			18	26	2xPWR	50 000	
Delta-I	1972–77	18	11 000			18	26	2xPWR	50 000	
Yankee-I	1967–77	16	9 600			18	27	2xPWR	50 000	
Hotel-III	1958–62	1	6 500			20	25	2xPWR	30 000	2x80
SSGN										
Oscar	1978–	4(1)	16 000			16	35	2xPWR	90 000	
Papa	1969–71	1	8 000			16	39	2x?	60 000–75 000	
Charlie-II	1973–80	6	5 500			16	23	1xPWR	15 000	2x80
Charlie-I	1967–73	10	4 800			16	23	1xPWR	15 000	2x80
Echo-II	1961–67	29	6 200			20	23	2xPWR	30 000	
Yankee	1983 conv		13 650				23	2xPWR	35 000	
SSN										
Akula	1984–	4+1	8 000	840			42+	2xPWR	60 000	2x120
Mike	1983	(0)	9 700	6–700	900		36–38	2xPWR	47 000	
Alfa	1979–83	6	3 700	550			43–45	1xLMR	40 000	
Sierra	1983–	2+1	7 550	400	600		35	2xPWR	30 000	
Victor-III	1978–86	23	6 300	400			29	2xPWR	30 000	2x80
Victor-II	1972–78	7	5 700	400		20	30	2xPWR	30 000	2x80
Victor-I	1968–75	16	5 100				30–32	2xPWR	30 000	2x80
Echo-I	1960–62	5	5 500			20	25	2xPWR	30 000	2x80
November	1958–63	12	5 300				30	2xPWR	30 000	2x80
Yankee		2+13	13 650				23	2xPWR	35 000	2x80

Country Sub. type	Constr. time	Units	Displ. dived tons	Diving depths (m) Norm.	Max	Speed (kn) Surf.	div.	React. type	Power SHP	Mwatt	Refueling time (y)
Hotel-II	1958-62	6	6 500			20	25	2xPWR	30 000		
X-ray		1									
Uniform	1982	1	2 500								
United Kingdom											
SSBN											
Vanguard	1986–	(2)	15 000				25	PWR-2	22 500	130	8–9
Resolution	1964–69	4	8 500			20	25	PWR-1	15 000	70	
SSN											
Trafalgar	1978–	6(1)	5 200	>175			32	PWR-1	15 000	70	
Swiftsure	1969–81	6	4 900				30+	PWR-1	15 000	70	8–9
Valiant	1963–67	2	4 800				28	PWR-1	15 000	70	7
Churchill	1968–71	3	4 800				28	PWR-1	15 000	70	
SSN-20(W)	1990–		5 000					PWR-2	22 500	130	8–9
France											
SNLE-NG											
Le Triomphant	1986–	1(5)	14 200	>300			25	1 PWR	41 500		
SNLE											
L'Inflexible	1979	1	8 900	300			25	1 PWR	16 000		
Le Redoutable	1969–80	5	8 900	250				1 PWR	16 000		
SNA 72											
Rubis	1976–	6(2)	2 670	300				1PWR	9 500	48	

Table 15 Technical data on existing and planned nuclear submarines.

References

(1) Arkin, W.M. and J. Handler (1989) 'Naval Accidents 1945–1987', Green-peace/Institute of Policy Studies.
Bremer, Jens S. (1986) 'Soviet Submarine Accidents', *Navy International,* May 1986.
Maclean, Malcolm (1989) 'Naval Accident Losses, A 25-year History', *Navy International,* February 1989.
(2) Head Quarters Defence Command Norway (1990).
(3) *Jane's Defence Weekly* (1986) March 29th.
(4) Heggstad, K.M. (1983) 'Submarine Hulls of Titanium', *Maritime Defence,* April 1983.
(5) Cochran, Th.B. and W.M. Arkin (1987) *Nuclear Weapons Data Book,* Vol. II.
Norris, R.S. and M.M. Hoenig *US Nuclear Warhead Production,* Natural Resources Defence Council, Ballinger Publishing Company.
(6) 'NS Otto Hahn – Erstes Deutsches Kernenergieschiff' (1981) GKSS 81/E/20, Forschungszentrum Geesthacht.
(7) Kolstad, E., C. Vitanza and R.W. Miller (1980) 'Fuel Thermal Behaviour During Steady State and Transient Operating Conditions', HPR 239, OECD Halden Reactor Project.
(8) Børresen, Jacob (1985) 'USA-marinens Operasjoner i Nord-Atlanteren og Norskehavet', Norsk Utenrikspolitisk Institutt, No. 89, May 1985.
(9) *Jane's Defence Weekly,* August 29th, 1986.
(10) Horlick, T. (1982) 'Nuclear Submarine Propulsion in the RN', *Navy International,* March 1982.
(11) *Jane's Defence Weekly,* March 29th, 1986.
(12) Meason, J.E. (1988) 'Brazil's Plans to Build a Nuclear Submarine Industry', *Jane's Defence Weekly,* July 23rd, 1988.
(13) Hobson, S. (1988) 'Canada's Defence Rides on Election', *Jane's Defence Weekly,* October 8th, 1988.
(14) Heggstad, K.M. (1983) 'Submarine Hulls of Titanium', *Maritime Defence,* April 1983.
(15) 'Code of Safety for Nuclear Merchant Ships' (1982) International Maritime Organization, London.

(16) Rodinov, N., V. Vorobyer and F. Gabaydulin (1982) 'Technical Operation: New Addition to the Fleet: The Nuclear Powered Lighter Carrier', *Morskoy Flot*, No. 8, August 1982.

(17) 'NS Otto Hahn – Safety Assessment' (1968) Gesellschaft für Kernenergieverwertung in Schiffbau und Shiffahrt m.b.H., Forschungszentrum Geestacht.

(18) *Technical Safety Evaluation of the NS 'Savannah'* (1964) Euratom EUR 1621.c.

(19) *NS 'Savannah' Safety Assessment*, Vol. III (1961) US Atomic Energy Commission.

(20) House of Commons Defence Committee (1989) 'Decommissioning of Nuclear Submarines', 7th Report, Session 1988–1989, Her Majesty's Stationary Office, London.

(21) Cochran, Th.B. et al. (1987) *Nuclear Weapons Databook*, Vol. II, Natural Resources Defence Council.

(22) Cochran, Stephen G. (1987) 'Why Nuclear Testing Is Necessary: A Nuclear Weapon Scientist's Perspective', UCID-20878.

(23) Naval Safety Center. 'Submarine Force: Mishaps Statistical Summary, Calender Years 1983 thru 1987' (n.d.) (released under the Freedom of Information Act).

(24) Finke, G. (1984) *Fremdenergieunabhängiger Nachwärmeabfuhr aus Schiffskernreaktoranlagen im Sinkfall*, Forschungszentrum Geesthacht, GKSS 84/E/22.

(25) 'LOFT Core Damage Test Lauded' (1985) *Nuclear Engineering International*, Sept. 1985.

(26) Gittus, J.H. (ed.) (1982) *PWR Degraded Core Analysis*, ND-R-610(S), Springfields Nuclear Laboratory, United Kingdom Atomic Energy Authority.

(27) 'Methodology for Assessing Impacts of Radioactivity on Aquatic Ecosystems', *Panel Summary Report 1979*, p. 14. Technical Reports Series No. 190, International Atomic Energy Agency, Vienna.

(28) *Radioactivity in the Marine Environment* (1971), National Academy of Sciences, Washington DC.

(29) Christensen, G.C. (1984) 'Radioactivity in Fucus Vesiculosus Along the Norwegian North Sea and Skagerak Coast 1980–1983', IAEA Meeting, Helsinki.

(30) Aarkrog, A. (1977) 'Environmental Behaviour of Plutonium Accidentally Released at Thule (Greenland)', *Health Physics*, Vol. 32 (April), pp. 271–284.

(31) *Annual Report and Accounts*, British Nuclear Fuel plc 1987/88, Risley, Warrington.

(32) Dickson, R.R., E.M. Guitrowicz and A.J. Watson (1990) 'Deep-Water Renewal in the Northern North Atlantic', *Nature*, Vol. 344, April 26th, 1990.

(33) Hunt, G.C. (1988) 'Radioactivity in Surface and Coastal Waters of the British Isles 1987', Lowestoft, UK.

(34) Marietta M.G. and W.F. Simmons (1988) 'Dispersal of Radionuclides in

the Oceans: Modes, Data Sets and Regional Descriptions', Vol. 8, Nuclear Energy Agency, Paris.

(35) 'GESAMP: An Oceanographic Model for the Dispersion of Wastes Disposed of in the Deep Sea' (1983) *Reports and Studies,* No. 19, IAEA, Vienna.

(36) Nishiwaki, Y. (1981) 'Some Historical Background to the IAEA Definition and Recommendations Concerning High-Level Radioactive Wastes', IAEA-SM-248/117.

(37) 'The Radiological Basis of the IAEA Revised Definition and Recommendations Concerning High-Level Radioactive Waste Unsuitable for Dumping at Sea', IAEA-211, Vienna, 1978.

(38) *Review of the Continued Suitability of the Dumping Site for Radioactive Waste in the North-East Atlantic,* Nuclear Energy Agency (OECD), Paris, 1985, p. 229.

(39) 'Decommissioning of Nuclear Submarines' (1989) Defence Committee Seventh Report, Her Majesty's Stationary Office, London.

(40) Prandle, D. (1984) 'A Modelling Study of the Mixing of Caesium-137 in the Seas of the European Continental Shelf', *Philosophical Transactions of the Royal Society,* A 310, London.

(41) Dahlgaard et al. (1984) 'Contaminant Fluxes through the Coastal Zone', Preprint Symposium, Nantes, May 1984.

(42) Aarkrog, A. (1971) 'Radiological Investigations of Plutonium in an Arctic Environment', *Health Physics,* Vol. 20, Jan. 1971, p. 31.

(43) Aarkrog, A. (1984) 'Further Studies of Plutonium and Americium at Thule (Greenland)', *Health Physics,* Vol. 46, 1984.

(44) Noshkin, V.E., K.M. Wong (1980) 'Plutonium Mobilization from Sedimentary Sources to Solution in the Environment', *Marine Ecology Seminar,* Tokyo 1979, NEA, Paris, 1980.

(45) Pentreath, R.J. et al. (1979) 'Alpha-Emitting Nuclides in Commercial Fish Species Caught in the Vicinity of Windscale, UK, and Their Radiological Significance to Man', Proceedings of a Seminar, IAEA, Vienna.

(46) Clark, M.J. and G.A.M. Webb (1980) 'A Model to Assess Exposure from Releases of Radioactivity into the Seas of Northern Europe', Procedings IAEA, Vienna.

Index

Acknowledgements

The figures below have been reproduced with kind permission from the following sources:

Figs. 2, 3, 4, 5, 6 and 8: Head Quarters Defence Command Norway.

Fig. 12: C.C. Horton: 'Submarine Nuclear Power Plants', *The Nuclear Engineer,* vol. 25, No. 1 Jan.–Febr. 1984, p. 4.

Figs. 13 and 15: 'E. Olderins Orientering om utländska ubåtar, Navalatom 1960', in *Mobila Kärnenergiaggregat,* by Bengt Andersson, FAO Report C 20743-4.1 November 1988, pp. 10–11.

Figs. 14, 16, 17 and 20: 'NS Otto Hahn – Erstes Deutsches Kernenergischiff', GKSS 81/E/20, pp. 40, 144 and 189. (Published by GKSS-Forschungszentrum Geesthacht.)

Fig. 28: Kåre M. Heggstad: 'Submarine Pressure Hulls', *Maritime Defence,* April 1983.

Figs. 37 and 38: 'Feasibility of Disposal of High-Level Radioactive Waste into the Seabed', *OECD Report* vol. 8, pp. 51–52.

Fig. 39: Derrick Ballongton, *Jane's Defence Weekly,* vol. 5, No. 19, p. 865, 17 May 1986.

Figs. 40, 41 and 42: G.J. Hunt: 'Radioactivity in Surface and Coastal Waters off the British Isles, 1987', *Aquatic Environment Monitoring Report,* No. 19, Published by the Ministry of Agriculture, Fisheries and Food, Suffolk, England 1988.

Fig. 43: David Prandle: 'A Modelling Study of the Mixing of Cs-137 in the Seas of the European Continental Shelf', *Phil. Trans. Royal Soc.,* London, A 310, 1984, p. 430.

Fig. 45: 'Methodology for Assessing Impacts of Radioactivity on Aquatic Ecosystems', *Technical Reports Series* No. 190, 1979, p. 14, IAEA, Vienna.